# GOOD CAMEL, GOOD LIFE

# GOOD CAMEL, GOOD LIFE

## FINDING ENLIGHTENMENT ONE DROP OF SWEAT AT A TIME

### Scott Bischke

MountainWorks Press

Other books by Scott Bischke

CROSSING DIVIDES
A Couples' Story of Cancer, Hope, and
Hiking Montana's Continental Divide
(American Cancer Society 2002)

TWO WHEELS AROUND NEW ZEALAND
A Bicycle Journey on Friendly Roads
(Pruett Publishing hardback 1992; Ecopress paperback 1996)

GOOD CAMEL, GOOD LIFE
Finding Enlightenment
One Drop of Sweat at a Time

Copyright © 2010 by Scott Bischke

ISBN 978-0-9825947-0-4

Library of Congress Catalog Number: 2010900083

Publisher—MountainWorks Press

An imprint of MountainWorks, Incorporated

Yoga illustrations courtesy of Randee Brinks
of Bikram Yoga Abbortsford, British Columbia—
see www.bikramyogaabbotsford.com.

Chasing rabbit illustration adapted from Wikipedia public files.

Bikram Choudhury quotes taken from Bikram Yoga by Bikram
Choudhury, HarperCollins 2007, unless otherwise noted.

*To order books see on-line retailers (and write reviews!),*
*your local bookstore, or www.emountainworks.com/books.*
*Also, be sure to look for us on FaceBook.*

For my
Mother and Father

In thanks for the endless examples
they have provided me on how to
live a good Life

# Contents

# BEFORE

# Chapter 1

# Choosing to Breathe

*Breathing in I say,*
*"Thank you for being alive today."*
*Breathing out I say,*
*"Help me to appreciate each moment."*

—Thich Nhat Hahn

I was lollygagging again—taking photos, looking for bison, marveling at patches of golden aspens on sunlit hillsides. Ah, the sweet joy that is Yellowstone in the fall. Not a soul about, just the murmur of a gentle breeze moving across sagebrush steppe.

We had hiked in barely a half mile from the road, but my wife Kate and our friend Jennifer were already 100 yards ahead. A couple miles beyond them stood Electric Peak, covered in the year's first snow, a cold contrast to the warm September day yet an undisputable sign of the icy months to come. At that moment animals throughout Yellowstone were preparing for winter: elk and bison moving to lower grounds where snowpack would be slimmer and graze more plentiful; Clark's Nuthatches hiding pine seeds to eat during the cold months; geese and swans flying off to warmer lands to the south; bears gorging themselves for the long hibernation ahead.

The previous night Kate, Jennifer, and I had decided to go on the hike. We had agreed that there would be no problem waiting until 9:30, until after my 8 AM yoga class, before departing Bozeman for the Park. Thus while Kate and Jennifer read the paper and drank morning espressos, I was turning and twisting and sweating, listening to my instructor talk about using my breath to calm my fears and reconnect my body and mind.

They picked me up out front of the studio and we drove 90 minutes to the north entrance of Yellowstone. Our plan was to enjoy a quiet walk from near Bunsen Peak out across Swan Flats and then down to the magnificent travertine terraces of Mammoth Hot Springs.

It was a great plan, but if I kept taking photos and reveling in the moment Kate and Jennifer would beat me to the Terraces by two hours. So I jogged a bit to rejoin my hiking mates, catching them just as they disappeared over a hill. As I slipped over the crest, suddenly they both turned back toward me, walking with great intent and purpose. As Kate glanced over her shoulder Jennifer said, "Grizzly— there's a big grizzly beside the trail."

My first reaction was to bolt. Less than heroic, I know, but I have a fear of grizzlies that at times can be gut-wrenching. Perhaps that doesn't sound unusual. But interestingly after decades of walking through grizzly country I've come to realize that the fear is always strongest when I am only imagining the bear's presence—

say a noise outside the tent at 3 AM. I've learned that it is the fear of the unknown, far more than fear of the bear, that grabs me.

So instead I took a deep breath.

Fear can sometimes cloud reality. Imagined fear emanates from the mind, and I have worked for years to learn to control it. Much of my yoga practice—including just a couple hours earlier that very morning—has spoken to using the breath to control the mind, to gain peace and find centeredness, and to overcome life's challenges and fears.

I took another breath.

This goal of controlling the mind in the face of fear is reflected in the words of the eighth century Buddhist master Shantideva, who said[1],

> If this elephant of mind is bound on all sides
> by the cord of mindfulness,
> All fear disappears and complete happiness comes.
> All enemies: all the tigers, lions, elephants, bears, serpents...;
> All of these are bound by the mastery of your mind,
> And by the taming of that one mind, all are subdued....

I took a third breath, then walked forward to join my two compatriots for a look at the bear. As so many times before, knowing that the grizzly was actually there, not some made up boogey man of the mind, turned the situation concrete and far less fearful. I stepped past Kate.

The big grizz stood in the sage brush perhaps 70 yards

---

[1] As quoted by Sogyal Rinpoche in The Tibetan Book of Living and Dying.

away. It was a large boar with a shoulder hump that jutted out prominently as it rooted around, head down. From our vantage we could not see the object of the bear's attention, but its behavior signaled the real possibility that it was feeding on a carcass, perhaps bison carrion or an elk calf that it had killed. The bear looked up once directly at us and then went back about his business, showing no indication of being agitated that we were invading his space.

The three of us took a collective deep breath, slipped back over the hill, and decided it best to hike somewhere else for the day.

A friend of mine once wrote that life is full of challenges, those that we choose and those that are thrust upon us. I know a bit about how challenges can be thrust upon us—possibly you do, too—in my case because of my wife Kate's bouts with cancer, recurrent cancer, and the remnant physical difficulties resulting from cancer treatment. We were once told that she would die within a year, a declaration that Kate *chose* not to accept.

Likewise my father would never have chosen Parkinson's Disease to be the defining challenge of the last part of his life. Like Kate, my father has fought with his disease, giving ground only grudgingly, seeking life first. Unlike cancer, however, where death so often seems to loom ever close, Parkinson's creeps insidiously into the fabric of day to day life, demanding ever more and more recognition until it is the core life experience for patient and family.

And indeed such health challenges do impact not just

the patient but the family, as well. Based on love there is no choice as to whether I will be an active part in caring for my wife. She is my favorite hiking partner, best friend, companion, and lover and I will do everything I can to help her when she needs me because I know she will do the same if the tables someday turn. Likewise I will always support my Mom and Dad when they need me in whatever way possible. They *already* have done the same for me.

Those are challenges *thrust* into my family's life. But in our affluent Western society, we are often privileged to *choose* some of our life challenges. Here I am thinking of challenges outside those resulting from our profession, concentrating more on those trials to which we voluntarily submit ourselves. Many such challenges are athletic— consider the marathoner or perhaps the swimmer at a masters' meet. Others are tied to challenging ourselves in nature—consider the backcountry skier or the big wall rock climber. Still other challenges might be more artistic or cerebral in design—consider the belly dancer or someone who has set themselves to read the classics.

I've been privileged enough through my years to choose to take on a number of such voluntary challenges. As a group these experiences make up the most memorable, vibrant, life-affirming moments of my life to date.

What would you remember if I asked you to name that time when you felt most alive? For me the answer would be easy: walking from Canada to Mexico along the Continental Divide Trail—roughly 3000 miles, five states, five years, two to three months each summer carrying a backpack with little else to think about besides staying dry, a soft place to sleep, my next drink of water, and how much food we had left before the next pickup.

For you the answers might be far different. Being a parent... active duty in the military...caring for an ailing loved one... serving your church community...time as a Peace Corps volunteer. Whatever they are, I think that the times we all feel most alive have this in common: *we have passion for the cause.*

Along with passion, two other common threads weave together the memories that make up those times *I* felt most alive: time and physicality.

The first, time, is a commodity we all believe is in too short supply. It's been said that time is nature's way of making sure that everything doesn't happen at once. Yet it seems our lives today are set up to make just the opposite occur: who ever has enough time to handle everything life throws our way? Kids, work, travel, volunteer activities.... The list never ends. No sooner do we cross one item off the list than three more get added.

But does it have to be so? My most life-affirming experiences had a common aspect—Kate and I chose to give ourselves the gift of time. We made sure no jobs called. We fully committed to be present in our times of travel and exploration. For me, the mental freedom afforded by unscheduled time is an unparalleled gift. Never are my thoughts more clear and substantial, my creativity more keen, than when my mind is emptied of its inventory of "to-dos".

This clarity of thought can be a step on the path

towards enlightenment; towards realizing that our potential
is limitless; towards, as Sogyal Rinpoche defines as the
central truth in Buddhist teaching, an awareness "that we
are already essentially perfect." But there is a key: *we must
actively participate to achieve this awareness.* Through what we
do; through the time we give ourselves. If we do not
participate, awareness is lost. As Sogyal Rinpoche notes,

> *Sometimes when the cell door is open,
> the prisoner chooses not to escape.*

My life-affirming experiences, those times when I
have felt closest to unraveling my own mysteries, have all
been strongly physical in nature. Sol Luckman has written
that "True enlightenment, in addition to being a mental
state, appears to have *physical* consequences." My sense is
that the opposite is also true: rigorous physical effort
engenders enlightenment. In this harried life of day-to-day
chores how different it is to instead be forced to worry
about a painful blister, the lack of water in the desert, the
grizzly bear along the trail.

Why is it, by the way, that our senses become more
acute in grizzly country? Suddenly my mind registers faint
new smells and my ears pick up the sound of breaking
twigs. Demanding physical activity helps us to remove the
frivolous from our minds and focus on the fundamental,
leading to improved awareness of self, and improved
awareness of the world around us.

I find that yoga helps me in the same way.

K ate and I started yoga in the mid-90s as part of our healing after the radiation, chemotherapy, and the many surgeries associated with her recurrent cancer. We came to yoga innocently enough. Hewlett-Packard, in Corvallis Oregon where we lived and worked at the time, offered on-site yoga as part of its employee health and wellness plan. An hour to walk across the HP campus and decompress at lunch? And free? Super, sign me up.

HP contracted with a wonderful teacher, Sujita, who introduced us to "tree" yoga—a rhythmic, flowing, almost dance-like combination of yoga postures interspersed with breathing and focus exercises. I never did get the tree aspect of the yoga; I kept waiting for imagery about putting down strong roots and bearing fruit. It's only recently that I've come to the realization that it was most likely TriYoga®, a style of yoga popularized by yogini Kali Ray.

I wasn't too mindful in my early yoga days.

Regardless of my lack of understanding about just what I was doing, I found Sujita endlessly inspirational—to learn from, to listen to, to watch. She twisted and turned and moved her body in ways that seemed illegal. And she periodically worked me into knots I was unsure I would ever untie from. I'd simply lay there like a toasted pretzel until sometime before the end of class Sujita would come by to help me untangle my arms and legs and regain some sense of dignity. I always left class feeling happy that I survived, and—I soon came to realize—feeling a bit better physically and mentally than when I arrived.

Sujita tolerated me for several years until Kate and I

left HP and moved home to Montana. Years passed in Bozeman. I retained my interest in yoga but found no outlet for it. That is right up until I heard rumor of a new studio opening in town to be run by friends of friends, plus rumored to be a *hot* studio. I'd never heard of such a thing before. My interest was piqued.

I've always been a masochist for heat and exercise. I live for 99 °F runs in August. So not only didn't heat scare me, it sounded *good*.

I met Chris and Rebekah, the owners of the new studio, through our mutual friends long before I ever stepped into one of their classes. Chris is on the lanky side, with little hair and often a devil-may-care look about him. Rebekah is dark haired with beautiful eyes and apple cheeks. Both exude wellness and vitality, with ready and vibrant smiles.

Early on as we were getting to know them, Kate and I canoed a remote Montana river with Chris and Rebekah, along with many other friends. Four days and three nights through some of the most beautiful country you could ever want to see: deep forest, towering sunset-orange cliffs, icy springs pouring from the hillsides, mostly clear blue skies. Mostly clear blue, that is, except for the first day when freezing rain sent us all into slickers and under tarps. In the morning, with everything sodden and most everyone holding on to hot coffee and wrapped in every piece of clothing they could find, I noticed Chris standing off to the side away from the main group.

Chris stood with his feet together, hands clasped under his chin. He brought his elbows together in front of

himself, then inhaled a single
breath, deeply and slowly. At
the same time he raised his
elbows while keeping his head in
position, looking straight ahead.
From the look on his face, the
rest of us seemed not to exist.
At the end of the breath Chris paused, his arms now lifted
outward like chicken wings but knuckles still under his
chin. Next he began to slowly exhale, forearms, elbows,
and wrists coming directly in front of his face, forearms
parallel to the ground, knuckles still under the chin, face
now turned up to the sky. Several times he repeated the
exercise, and each time I watched with great interest.

At that moment I had barely heard the name "Bikram"
and certainly did not recognize Chris's actions to be
*Pranayama* breathing, the first breathing exercise in Bikram
Choudhury's yoga sequence. I did not know that Chris and
Rebekah's studio was part of a worldwide yoga movement,
nor did I know that the movement centered around one
man from India and his singular vision of bringing yoga to
the masses of the West.

At that moment I only knew I was intrigued.

# DURING

ᛁ᚛ᚾ.. ᚦ ᚱ ᚨ.. ᛁ    Chapter 2

# Warming to the Challenge

*If I have the belief that I can do it,
I shall surely acquire the capacity to do it
even if I may not have it at the beginning.*

—Ghandi

P icture yourself in Phoenix...or Calcutta...
standing on a cement sidewalk with the sun high
overhead. It is 105 °F and you are sweating. Now—
especially if you are in Phoenix—add some humidity, lots
of humidity. Think Bangkok humidity. Think sweltering,
stifling, oxygen-robbing humidity.

Now surround yourself with 30 other sweating souls.
And picture this—they are naked, or nearly so. But it
doesn't really matter. So are you.

Now begin to contort your body in all shapes and
manners that until this very moment you never felt any
compelling reason to attempt, much less to achieve. Your
back hurts like hell, you lie down because you feel like

fainting, and you can't get the burning sweat out of your eyes.

You think about just stopping but then realize that you can't. Why? Because there is a gorgeous, hard bodied creature in front of you barking orders. The instructor. And for a reason that is becoming foggier as the postures go by, you have agreed to listen. Hell, you've even paid to let them do this to you.

And, it should be noted, *you well need to listen.* It seems that most of the directions and corrections are aimed at you.

The postures continue. Your back still hurts but it matters less and less now because so do your neck, your hips, and your knees. In fact the pain is actually becoming more bearable because it is hard to focus on just one throbbing body part. Everything now hurts.

Gee, maybe blacking out at this point wouldn't be such a bad idea....

OK, now let's pick up the entire show—all 32 sweaty bodies—and drop them into a shoebox yoga studio no bigger than the average living room. It's just as hot...and humid. Sweltering, stifling, oxygen-robbing humidity.

Look around you. Close, those people are now *ever so close* to you. Almost touching you. And they're still sweaty and nearly naked.

And now look ahead. Try not to be startled. Directly in front of you, staring right back at you, is you. Sweaty...nearly naked...you. Full bore in the mirror six feet away. You cannot hide and it is far too late to run— quick, get ready now, the next posture is starting.

Welcome, my friends, you have arrived at Bikram's Torture Chamber.

B ikram Choudhury was born in 1946 in Calcutta, in the state of Bengal, India, where as a young child two of his siblings died in a smallpox epidemic. Hoping to find solace for his grieving wife, Bikram's father moved the family to Deoghar in the state of Bihar. In his book <u>Bikram Yoga</u>, Bikram says that the move proved fateful for his later life—as a preschooler he received his first yoga lessons from an old master. The seven-day-per-week instruction included the learning and daily practice of 84-yoga *asanas* (postures). Bikram admits he did not know that he was learning *asanas* at the time; he was simply in it for the candy reward.

The family returned to Calcutta in his sixth year and again, rather serendipitously, he ran into another old master, Bishnu Charan Ghosh, at a neighborhood gymnasium. Ghosh was to become, in Bikram's words,

*...my guru and the greatest influence in my life. I remained at his side, studied with him, and learned everything I know about yoga from him for the next 20 years. If you ask me today what it is that I do, I will tell you, "I practice my guru's wisdom."*

That wisdom did not come easily. Ghosh, who was at once a doctor, lawyer, professor, engineer, poet, philosopher and more, also took it upon himself to help street kids better themselves. Seeing the young man's ability to complete the *asanas*, Ghosh took Bikram under his wing and strengthened his mind and his body through yoga practice and weight lifting. The work was not easy, nothing short of perfection counted, and Ghosh utilized screaming as a major motivational tool. Not the only tool for motivation, however, as the guru also hung a large, sharp sword on the wall of the school and threatened to cut off his students' heads if he ever saw them not trying hard enough. As Bikram relates,

*When you are at the very brink of physical, mental, and emotional exhaustion, and some raving madman swinging a razor-sharp sword is screaming at you so loudly that your hair is blown back by the force of his voice, believe me, you listen. Now, every time I want to quit, compromise, or just get up and leave, my guru is there with his sword, acting like the angriest yogi on Earth. I miss him so much; you have no idea.*

At 13 years of age, Bikram became the youngest person ever to win the All-India Yoga *Asana* Championship. He won again at 14 and 15. He also became a proficient weight lifter, breaking records along the way, until one day his spotter dropped a 380-pound weight on his knee, crunching it miserably. One doctor told Bikram he would never walk again, another that the leg should be amputated, still another that he could rebuild the damaged knee with stainless steel. For months Bikram's sister carried him to the bathroom. Life was so desperate that he considered suicide.

The story of how Bikram healed his knee through yoga is part of the mythos that permeates Bikram Yoga classes. Instructor frequently say, "Yoga healed Bikram...", or perhaps "Bikram healed himself with yoga...". What I've never heard told in those stories is the credit Bikram gives to his guru for the healing. Instead of suicide, Bikram called on Ghosh:

> I limped back to him, and he saved me. He had two huge bodybuilders force my legs—including the shattered knee—into Lotus position. If you are familiar with this cross-legged position you know it requires great flexibility of the knees. The pain was unbelievable. I'd bite my finger or a stick, and I'd pass out. But after six months I could do it myself. It was nothing less than a miracle, and this inspired me to become a yoga teacher.

After his healing, Bikram began to help Ghosh with patients who came to him for healing of various physical ailments. This was ultra-poor India so expensive medicine or medical treatments were not an option. Instead, diet and yoga postures made up every treatment plan for curing the sick. Once Ghosh meted out the prescription, his disciples, including Bikram, would take the patient away to teach them the necessary yoga postures.

Later Ghosh sent Bikram to Bombay to heal through yoga on his own. But soon Bikram had more people—a hundred at a time—lined up than he could possibly treat, and he realized that if he gave them all individual attention he would only be able to treat 15 people a day! Yet many of them, he knew, had common ailments like diabetes, arthritis, and problems of the heart, thyroid, and nervous system. That is when, as Bikram says,

*I thought that if there was some way I could teach everyone the right postures in the correct order, no matter what their disease or condition, then I could teach in groups and help more people. If penicillin worked on so many kinds of infections, couldn't one yoga prescription be used that way, too? What's more, yoga would work as preventative medicine, as well.*

Thus inspired, Bikram began to develop his Sequence of 26 postures and two breathing exercises that he would bring to the masses as part of his Karma Yoga, his reason for being on Earth. Bikram says his guru Ghosh made it clear to him that, "…it's my job to help as many people as possible by sharing my Indian heritage and the wisdom passed down over the centuries."

Bikram selected the 26 postures from the 84 core Hatha yoga postures he learned from Ghosh. To make the selection, he worked through "…the laboratory of my own body…" to select postures that would "… systematically work every part of the body, to give all the internal organs, all the veins, all the ligaments, and all the muscles everything they need to maintain optimal health and maximum function".

Central to Bikram's Sequence was the decision to run his yoga classes at 105 °F. Why so hot? Bikram says that yoga changes the body from inside to outside, and to accomplish that change we need to heat the body up to soften it, "…because a warm body is a flexible body. Then you can reshape the body any way you want."

Ghosh was at first skeptical of Bikram's one-size-fits-all yoga Sequence as it must have seemed so contrary to the intimate interactions he usually had with his patients. Yet even he was eventually won over by the Bikram's enthusiasm.    Possibly Gosh also saw the wisdom in recognizing the difficulties in the numbers game that led Bikram to create his Sequence.

In his last days Ghosh said to Bikram, "Promise you will complete my incomplete job," meaning bringing yoga to the West and America. Bikram promised. The newly developed Sequence provided Bikram the tool he needed to achieve his guru's goal.

O ver 40 years after Bikram made his promise, I was at Bikram's Yoga College of India in Bozeman, upstairs in a restored brick building, 10,000 miles from Calcutta, working my way through the early stages of his Sequence. It was a Saturday morning in October, the end of my first week of the Bikram Challenge. Shortly after class, Kate and Jennifer would pick me up to go hike with a grizzly bear in Yellowstone.

I had been practicing Bikram Yoga regularly for roughly three years, averaging perhaps once a week, with a few ambitious weeks doing two classes. I had enough classes under my belt to know that to be ready for class all I needed was a yoga mat, a towel to cover that, a water bottle, and a pair of shorts.    And I pretty much had Bikram's Sequence locked into memory. Ninety minutes of heat and humidity; two breathing exercises and 26 postures:

## Standing Series

- o   Standing Deep Breathing exercise
- ❖   *Warm Up Series*
  1. Half Moon pose
  2. Hands to Feet pose
  3. Awkward pose
  4. Eagle pose

- ❖   *Standing One-legged Concentration Series*
  5. Standing Head to Knee pose
  6. Standing Bow Pulling pose
  7. Balancing Stick pose

  --------
  8. Standing Separate Leg Stretching pose
  9. Triangle pose
  10. Standing Separate Leg Head to Knee pose
  11. Tree pose
  12. Toe Stand pose

## Floor Series

  13. Dead Body pose
  14. Wind Removing pose
- ❖   *Spine Strengthening Series*
  15. Sit Up
  16. Cobra pose
  17. Locust pose
  18. Full Locust pose
  19. Bow pose

  --------
  20. Fixed Firm pose
  21. Half Tortoise pose
- ❖   *Final, deepest poses*
  22. Camel pose
  23. Rabbit pose
  24. Head to Knee pose

25. Final Stretching pose
26. Spine-Twisting pose
o    Blowing in Firm pose and Second Breathing exercise

Somewhere along the way—perhaps after he left India for Japan, then Hawaii, and eventually Los Angeles—Bikram began to say, "Give me your body for 60 days, and I will change your life". That saying, along with Bikram's belief that we should all practice yoga six-days per week, led to the creation of the Bikram Challenge.

The Bikram Challenge is, ostensibly, practicing six days a week for ten weeks, or 60 days out of 70. I say "ostensibly" because somehow the business juggernaut that is Bikram Yoga has *not* chiseled the definition of the Challenge onto a stone tablet the way it has the 26-posture Sequence and Dialogue that goes along with its teaching. Along with the 60-days-in-70 approach, 30 days in-a-row constitutes the Challenge for some studios, 40-days-in-60 for some others, 60 days straight with not a single day off for others, and for still others it is 60 days in "two months" (meaning, one must surmise, that you could have two days off if you picked July and August or only go for 59 days if you picked January and February).

When I first started thinking about the Challenge, I was happy Chris and Rebekah had settled on the 60-days-in-70 definition. I could be gone once a week, and they even allowed practicing twice a day if absolutely necessary to free up another day in the week. Chris explained that they preferred people not make use of the twice a day option. The idea here, after all, is to help you see how

your mind and body change if you create a consistent
practice. Still, he said, they understood that life sometimes
throws us curveballs we cannot foresee so they were
willing to bend a bit.

Life, indeed, was throwing Kate and me a curveball at
the moment, or maybe a high hard one would be a better
metaphor. The last six months had been tough on her,
tough on us. Kate had been in and out of the hospital a half
dozen times with issues associated with radiation damage
from cancer treatment a dozen years back.

In class that day I was in theory in the early stages of
my 60-day Bikram Challenge. The reason my 60-day
Challenge existed only "in theory" was our uncertainty over
Kate's future. Surgery had been scheduled in Portland
Oregon for early November, still a month away, and we
had no way of knowing whether her condition would allow
me to be available to meet the rigorous time requirements
of the Challenge.

C hallenge Week 1/Day 6. I was getting ready for
class at the end of my first of ten weeks of the
Challenge and struggling a bit. Six days of yoga in a row
was exactly five days more in a row than I had ever done
before. The small of my back hurt like hell and I was really
looking forward to a rest day. Mentally I continued to
worry about committing to the Challenge because of
uncertainties over Kate's health, but now after five days in
a row I also began to worry whether my body could take it.

Stepping into the Torture Chamber that day, feeling
the 105 °F heat pour over me as I closed the door on the

outside world, I declared then and there that I would not go for a long run on my rest day as I had initially planned. Instead a couch, a heating pad, a half dozen Advil, and a large glass of Cabernet now sounded far more attractive.

The studio in Bozeman is long and slim, with three brick walls and a long mirrored front wall. In one corner there is an interesting little jog, suitable for a single person, with its own front mirror three feet ahead. Three blue lines run across the length of the room to help students with alignment of their feet and optimal person-to-person separation.

I found an empty spot in front of the class, rolled out my yoga mat on the thin carpet, spread my towel on top of that, and lay down. The towel captures sweat as you practice. But on Day 6 I started sweating before we even got off the floor to start first breathing exercise, *Pranayama* Standing Deep Breathing, which I had watched Chris practice on our river trip.

Sweating this early, at least for me, is a poor sign akin to my body waving a white flag in surrender before we've even started. But when Rebekah entered the studio and asked us to all please stand, I arose to go ahead with Standing Deep Breathing anyway, like a lamb being led to slaughter.

This beginning breathing exercise helps you deepen the use of your lungs, thereby addressing respiratory issues. Bikram, whom I doubt has ever been accused of

understatement, once said, "If you have a tiny, Dixie cup
capacity now, soon you will have a big, fat rain barrel."
Instructors regularly claim that deep breathing also brings
oxygen to the body, thus stimulating the heart, mind, and
muscles. I believe it all—OK maybe not the rain barrel
part—but for me the posture most strongly signals
transition. It's here and now that I begin to let go of my
daily concerns and surrender to the idea that I have chosen
to take 90 minutes out of my day to dedicate to my body,
mind, and soul, to take 90 minutes to set aside worries of
the outside world.

I was glowing with sweat by the start of Half Moon,
first pose in the Warm Up Series. Happily, even on a bad
day Half Moon seems to work for me. My very first day in
class Rebekah had praised me for how well I had done
locking my arms overhead like a steeple, then leaning to the
side from the waist giving a decidedly…well…half moon
look. "Very nice, Scott," she said, "that's your signature
pose!"

So I handled Half Moon just fine but by Hands to Feet
pose any thought I had of surviving the day vanished.
Hands to Feet is a bit like touching your toes, though the
goal is to stand on your five fingers, which you have
somehow managed like a gorilla to cup under your heels
from the back. Ok,
now put your forehead
on your shins and
straighten your legs.
The visualization often
given is that you should

squeeze so tight you leave no room for light or air, in fact
that you should look like a Japanese ham sandwich. I have
never seen a Japanese ham sandwich, but after hearing it
described in almost every Bikram's class I have ever taken I
can guarantee you what I am ordering for lunch the first
time I step off the plane in Tokyo.

Sweat poured from my forehead onto the towel I
stood on. The moment I tried to lay my stomach on the
top of my thighs, per the Dialogue, was the moment that I
remembered I had eaten an oversized bean burrito for
lunch a couple hours earlier. My stomach, already bulging
with foodstuffs, had also started swelling with gas. Buckled
in half as I was, my crowded abdomen had nowhere else to
go but up, resulting in the collapse of my lungs. So I exited
the pose red-faced and coughing, like a guy just ripping a
plastic bag off his head, having not taken a breath for 30
seconds.

It didn't help that Putter, who had previously
completed his own Challenge and whom I had always
looked up to as one of "the regulars", was behind me.
Word had gotten out that I was going to do the Challenge
and folks in class had started encouraging me. After class
on Day 5, Putter had said sincerely, "Thanks for letting me
practice next to you today." Respect earned by *just the
thought* that I was going after the Challenge. Now there we
stood between poses, reflections close in the mirror, Putter
deep in meditation and me coughing, ready to pass out, and
still not entirely sure I was up to taking on the Challenge.

The instructors had their way with me, too. A day or
two earlier, auburn haired, always-a-smile Wendy yelled

out, "Woo-woo! I heard you're doing the Challenge—awesome!"

"Well, no I'm *just thinking* about it." Ugh, how awkward.

And speaking of awkward, the third pose—Awkward pose—is just that, awkward! The pose has three parts, the most onerous of which puts you on your tippy toes like a half-naked       ballerina.
Arms straight in front of you.    Feet, knees, and arms six inches apart. Heels directly behind your feet. Now sit down deeply...lean your upper body     backwards...butt

down...no, no not in the toilet...spine straight...chest up...stomach in...arms solid...elbows locked...five fingers together...up on your toes...higher...higher still...breathe easily...relax your face...soften your gaze...focus on yourself one point in the mirror.

So many commands.

So few of them registering.

In my feeble state I felt like a raw rookie relearning, as Bikram once said, that "...keeping all these different parts of your body in alignment is like herding wild monkeys."

The one command of the bunch that *does* always register with me in Awkward is the call to keep my hands, knees, and feet six inches apart. How could I forget the description that Susan, a petite dark haired instructor, provided one day? "OK time for Awkward pose," she said.

"Everyone—hands, knees, and feet six inches apart. If you don't know what that is, you can lean down with your two fists side-by-side and put them between your feet. That will get you about six inches. Funny thing, men *always* seem to think that six inches is a lot longer than women, but *we* know the score, don't we ladies?"

I tried to hold still at the end of Awkward, stomach gurgling, burning sweat dripping into my eyes, a large wet spot now on my towel at my feet as if I had peed my shorts.

Eagle pose next. If I can make it through this I'll be done with the warm-up, I can have some water, and then maybe, just maybe, I'll make it through class. So I wrapped my arms around each other and twisted them like ropes, then bent my knees, balancing on just one foot, wrapping the other leg over the first, ultimately seeking to wrap the foot all the way around the calf of the opposite leg...yes the one that my twisted body was  balanced upon. Oh yea, and once you get there you're also supposed both lean back *and* bend that balancing leg as deeply as possible so that you become the shortest person in the room.

Tough to visualize? Trust me, even tougher to accomplish.

I managed to make it through Day 6, but not without getting run over by the yoga truck. Some days the body just doesn't want to work. For me it most often has to do with lack of sleep, lack of hydration before class, or the state of my gastrointestinal system—full being a major problem, empty to the stomach lining being optimal. If any of these three are off, look out for the yoga truck—KABOOM! The collision manifests as nausea, weak limbs, a woozy light-headedness, and flushed skin that feels ready to burst into flames. It may not knock you to your knees, indeed sometimes you can make it through, but after class there is no question to you or anyone watching that you've been hit.

Though I got nailed by the yoga truck that day, I survived without kneeling or even lying down (your only real options for recovery short of leaving the room, which is highly discouraged). By the time we made it to final breathing I was truly *done*, stick-a-fork-in-him kind of done.

Rebekah turned down the lights after final breathing and then, instead of providing us some final thoughts as she often does as we lie face up in *Savasana* recovering, she asked us to sing Happy Birthday to someone in class. The studio is small, almost like an echo chamber. The words came out slowly, gently. When someone added sweet harmony and we all held the final note of the song, the room resonated with a beautiful sound akin to Buddha bells.

Outside in the waiting area, Rebekah did not ask me about the yoga truck, though I must have looked like death warmed over. Instead she handed me an envelope.

"What's this?" I asked.

"Your contract," she replied.

"Contract? My contract for what?"

She gave me that twinkling Rebekah smile, looking at me, I was thinking, as if she were looking at her one-year old son Eli. "Your contract for the 60-day Challenge. It gives the ground rules and expectations, but mostly it shows us both you've committed to yourself to do the Challenge."

Rebekah smiled again before turning to talk with someone else.

I gulped, then slipped quietly into the locker room, the envelope already soaked with the sweat of my hands.

# Achieving Balance
# & Concentration

*One thing is certain.*
*Whatever I do I must do with all my might,*
*and do it with the unmistakable belief*
*that pain and death are necessary,*
*if I am to become the person I was meant to be*
*on the day I was born.*

—George Sheehan

O nce in class Rebekah told us a story she had just read, a story of beginnings.  She, like many Bikram's instructors, often shares things happening in her life, stories of recent workshops, quotes of wisdom, poetry, and jokes. On this day she told us a story about a butterfly.

It seems one day a man saw a small caterpillar beginning to weave its cocoon in the crook of a dead branch.  The next day the man came back to find the caterpillar fully encased in a white silk.  There was no movement; nothing to signify life. Day after day the man returned, never seeing any outward change in the cocoon. Weeks passed and the man became impatient. Finally one day he saw movement through the thin wall of the cocoon. The man was ecstatic, beyond himself at this sign of life. The man picked up the dead stick and poked a small hole in the cocoon, then blew warm air onto it for an hour. Encouraged by the warmth, the butterfly soon broke the hole open wide and climbed unsteadily out onto the dead branch. It tried to fan its wings but was too weak. In moments the butterfly fell from its precarious perch, dead from the cold and lack of strength.

"The lesson," Rebekah tells us, "is that we must be patient and emerge to reach our full potential on our own time, not someone else's."

S taggering out of class on Week 1/Day 6 of my Challenge, I think I felt a bit like Rebekah's shaky butterfly, unsure if my time for the Challenge had really come. I took a day off to recover, and spent some time considering comments I'd heard from other students who had completed the Challenge. One student told me that his body only rebelled during his third week. Another student told me that he had been hit by the yoga truck multiple times at the beginning, middle, and end of his Challenge. Still another student, who had just completed day 55 of his Challenge, said he'd thrown up six times after class already. From the looks of him in the locker room that day, number seven was coming at any moment.

Even as doubts swirled about in my mind, so did

altruistic thoughts about my ability to overcome the difficulties inherent in the Challenge and eventually triumph. Deep inside I had come to the Challenge hoping to improve my body, mind, and soul. I hoped that I would gain confidence, become a better person, find some sort of centeredness, show myself that I could do anything I set my mind to do.

OK, I plead guilty to being an unrelenting romantic. I think we *need* challenges in our lives. Too often we become stale. And stagnation kills. Just ask George Sheehan, the running guru, who in the last days of his life penned a beautiful book called <u>Going the Distance: One Man's Journey to the End of His Life</u>. With his cancer spreading and robbing him of his ability to run, and then to walk, Sheehan wrote succinctly, "Living is motion."

Sheehan's "motion", I would submit, can be taken figuratively as well as literally. Yes we need to challenge ourselves physically to make sure our muscles, tendons, and bones can still pull our bodies up to new heights. But we must also keep moving mentally to climb out of lives that have become too easy and comfortable for real accomplishment, lives where the mystery and challenge are gone and we don't even know where to look to find them, and thereby to find ourselves.

Writer Colin Fletcher, well known as a long-distance walker but a rookie to whitewater rafting, based his solo raft journey down the length of the Colorado River on just my kind of altruism. At the start of his journey it was apparent that he had a clear vision of what was really at stake:

*I needed something to pare the fat off my soul, to scare the
shit out of me, to make me grateful, again, for being
alive...If you are going to attempt long solo journeys you
had better, for safety's sake, be a realist; but at root you must
also be an unreasoning optimist... [I]n the end, such a
journey can restore an understanding of how insignificant
you are—and thereby set you free.*

And so, with such thoughts bouncing about in the
vacuous space between my ears, I headed back to the studio
for Week 2 of the Challenge, my mind refocused on the
prize.

B Ikram's big prize came from a most unlikely
benefactor. You see he credits his yoga empire
to Richard Milhouse Nixon. Well almost. He does credit
Tricky Dick with getting him to the United States where
Bikram could pursue his promise to his guru Ghosh to bring
yoga to the West and America.

Bikram set up two highly successful yoga studios in
Tokyo in the early 1970s after leaving India, along the way
healing Kakuei Tanaka of cerebral thrombosis. That's the
same Kakuei Tanaka who later became Japanese Prime
Minister, the one best known for taking a $4.5 million
bribe that led to his downfall, so it's apparent that in those
days Bikram was already moving in well-heeled, if not
always well-behaved, circles.

At some point Bikram started teaching yoga in Hawaii,
as well. For a time he commuted across the Pacific. On
one of his travels to Oahu he was met by the Governor of
Hawaii and spirited away to meet then President Nixon.

Nixon, who learned of Bikram from Mr. Tanaka, was suffering from painful thrombophlebitis[2]. Bikram provided Nixon a hydropathic therapy of yoga carried out in the bathtub filled with Epsom salts.

Nixon was healed. In appreciation he gave Bikram a green card to live permanently in the United States, which is exactly what Bikram did, moving to Los Angeles in 1973.

"Lock your knee, Scott," Jackie is saying, "lock your knee, lock your knee. Lock it up and throw away the key. Your knee is solid, one piece, like a lamp post. You have *no* knee." We are in the Standing One-legged Concentration Series attempting Standing Head to Knee pose. I am struggling to, you guessed it, lock my knee. I have come to Bikram Yoga 142 times at this point and exactly 142 times I have been told directly—no class-wide instruction here—that I really need to lock my knee or that my pose hasn't even started.

I am on Week 2/Day 11 of the Challenge. Kate has been feeling almost continually ill, meaning that my Challenge might end in a heartbeat if she needs me. The agonizing pain in my lower back has receded and much to my happy surprise the first four days of Week 2 have been easier than the final day of Week 1.

With the warm-up complete, the Standing One-legged Concentration Series is where the true work of class

---

[2] Thrombophlebitis is a swelling of a vein caused by a blood clot, most often occurring in the legs, and a potential precursor to pulmonary embolism, heart attack, or stroke. I must admit to being old enough to recall when Nixon's bout with phlebitis made the national news.

begins. It is the rare day that I am not already sweating by this point, but if not I can guarantee that perspiration will be beading up on my shoulders and forehead within ten seconds of starting Standing Head to Knee.

Here's why the pose is so tough. You start with feet together, then shift your weight to your left foot and *lock the knee*. Next you lift your right knee high, balancing on the left leg, then round over, reach out with both hands clasped, grabbing the right foot three inches below the toes, all ten fingers interlaced, holding on tight, and looking at your face or solid knee in the mirror. Now just hold it. The posture goes for a minute, that's 60 full, hot seconds, and you are only through part one. For those who are able (those who aren't are told to stay in part one, working on the locked knee), raise the right leg to fully extended and at a 90° angle with the left leg, both knees now locked, with toes flexed back toward your face, still with fingers interlaced below the toes. Got that? If so, you can bend your elbows and pull the foot and toes toward you with all your might, the elbows pointing down at the floor and below the calf muscle. Got that, too? *Really?* Both legs locked and all muscles taut? Great, but you're not done yet. Bend your torso forward,  keeping all else the same, tuck your chin to your chest and voila(!), finally touch your forehead to your knee. Oh...and hold it for a while, OK? Now repeat on the other side and then repeat both sides for a second set.

No problem boss!

Bikram is adamant that if you do not lock the knee, if the knee bends in the slightest, you get *no* benefit from the pose and actually risk injury. And that's not all:

*...if you cannot lock the knee, you won't ever find Self-Realization. People say that I am a hard-ass teacher, and it's true. But in this class and in life, you have to experience hell on Earth so that you may eventually reach heaven. Struggle instills discipline, so we can control our minds. Suffering breeds compassion. It sounds simplistic, but until you've actually stood on your own leg with your knee safely and powerfully locked like a solid piece of concrete, truly believing that you don't even have a knee, you won't be able to find inner peace, love, and happiness. This is why I always have to scream at my students to push them toward this goal. I tell my students, "When you die, I will jump up and down on your grave, shouting, 'Lock the damn knee!'"*

And so it is I learn that finding my true enlightenment has become intimately tied to locking my sorry knee while standing in front of a mirror sweating and nearly naked. I want to tell my friends that I have come to this discovery, but worry they will tell me that I really need to start getting out more.

Standing Bow Pulling pose comes next. Done correctly the pose looks ever so much like an archer pulling a bow tight. But here's an even easier image: start with a female Olympic skater wearing a one of those short, sequined skirts. Now picture the part where she reaches back and grabs the blade of her skate and lifts her foot high above her head, kicking with all her might. Simultaneously our skating friend lowers her abdomen and chest to parallel to the ground, arm reaching far forward in perfect alignment to her body. Beautiful. Elegant. Some call it the standing splits.

Now put the hand to the ankle instead of the skate, take away the ice and add stifling heat, and subtract a few pieces of clothing (and you thought figure skaters didn't wear much!), and more or less you've got Standing Bow pose. By the way, for the first round Bikram has you hold it for 60 seconds, longer than any Olympian I've ever watched.

And guess what? That single leg anchoring you to the floor is supposed to be locked (L-O-C-K-E-D, locked!). On this day I finally "get it" and hold the pose with a solid knee, not lifting my leg terribly high, but I am excited to see my foot barely rising above my head in the mirror. I lower my gaze to look into my eyes, then begin concentrating directly on my forehead. I push harder into my foot and extend my arm to touch the mirror, exactly as I have been instructed many times. For a moment I am in perfect balance and my breath comes easily. For once the 60 seconds seems doable. I am floating and centered. I feel happy, blissful, and admittedly perhaps even a bit smug as in the periphery people all around me are falling out of the pose.

But my self-satisfied reverie is short lived. "Your foot should be rising up above your head with everything else in a single line—your knee and shoulder should be hidden behind your body," Jackie is telling us all. Then I sense her turning to face me and suddenly hear her call out, "Scott, you need to pull your knee in.   Quit peeing on the hydrant!"

Yoga has a way of dashing the ego, forcing humbleness upon us.

We move on to Balancing Stick pose.   Once more balancing on and concentrating on the single locked leg. Our arms are stretched straight up behind our ears, fingers interlaced over our heads, index fingers released and pointing skyward like a steeple.   Jackie instructs us to stretch our upper body backward, then take a big step forward with our right leg.   "Now with no hesitation— BOOM!—half a second, drop your arms, body, legs into one line parallel the floor.   It's only a ten second pose, GO! If you wait it's over, you missed it.   Remember, hesitation is devastation."

The hands are forward, the head tilted up to look in the mirror, the entire body one solid piece, muscles tight from fingertips to toes.   Think of it, Bikram says, as a tug of war between two people pulling on your outstretched hands and foot, and leaving your body in a perfect T-shape. The trick is to hold that posture, even for a measly ten seconds.   It takes balance, with minute adjustments for body control, and it takes unwavering concentration.  Lose your concentration, lose your pose and you may find yourself, as I have, crashing into the front mirror, leaving an unsightly sweat streak for all to view.

In Balancing Stick you lower

your heart below your hips, thereby sending blood rushing to the heart. The idea, according to Bikram, is to give yourself an "intentional heart attack", making your heart stronger, so that you won't have the real kind later. "Better than a runner's sprint," Jackie claims. By the time we've completed both sides I can attest to her assertion; my heart is racing.

C oncentration, one of Bikram's five elements of a strong mind[3], is key to the Standing One-Legged Series. Balance alone will not suffice because it is so easy to be distracted by the heat, the sweat, and the discomfort that you can quickly fall out of the postures. Bikram, speaking of the conditions imposed by the Torture Chamber, says,

> *After you learn to discipline your body and mind under these conditions, you will truly be able to concentrate; no external will be able to break your powerful focus...That's concentration power, my friend. When you have it, no one can steal your peace.*

I know Bikram's words to be true. In class I find joy in for once concentrating on a single task and then committing to completing it before doing anything else. I love the focus required to hold a pose. Indeed, Bikram says that the ancient gurus created yoga as a way to prepare the body for an extended time sitting in meditation. Through the postures the ancients realized that if they could improve

---

[3] The others are faith, self-control, determination, and patience.

their power of concentration, they might be able to recognize and achieve their "Karma Yoga".

Karma Yoga, per Bikram, is the reason each of us was put here on Earth. Our job is to work to fulfill this destiny, but, as he says, "You must do it honestly, trying the right way, and you must do it on time, before you die."

To my way of thinking my Karma Yoga must emanate from my core beliefs. Several years back I attended a workshop where the leader asked us to concisely write down our strongest convictions. Five minutes. The idea, I think, is that the words right off the top should be an honest reflection of your true being, your reason for being on Earth. I found my scrawled note recently. Here's what I had come up with:

> *I believe that wilderness has the power to touch*
> *the soul of mankind,*
> *that strengthening the physical body enlivens*
> *and opens the mind,*
> *and that peace, joy, hope, and—ultimately—love*
> *are all that really matter.*

What are your core beliefs? What must you do before you die?

# Mirrors

*Just as you see yourself in a mirror,*
*Form and reflection look at each other.*
*You are not the reflection*
*Yet the reflection is you.*

—Tosan

H ave you ever set two large mirrors face-to-face? Reflections bounce back and forth and back and forth. Objects get smaller and smaller and more and more distant until they almost seem to disappear. But they don't disappear. Look deeper and there is always another object...and then another...and then yet another.

Mirrors have the power to make our world seem large and never ending.

Seeing double mirrors like that I'm always drawn to be part of that endless continuum, that visible manifestation of infinity. But you can't. When you step in between the mirrors you block the reflection. Suddenly it is only you...and you. It doesn't matter if you turn around, it is still just you.

Mirrors can do that, as well. They can make our world seem small and intimate.

Bikram has said that yoga allows you to introduce yourself "...to yourself, the person you never knew." Surely the mirror on the front wall of every Bikram's studio provides the gateway, at least the physical gateway, to that introduction.

Some folks run from the mirror, always setting their mat and towel as far away as possible so that their vision of themselves is not only distant, but also often partially blocked by other students. Not me. I like to be as close as possible, so close that when I swing my arms drops of sweat splatter on the mirror. I like to see my pudgy Buddha belly so I can keep that vision in my head for later when the siren song of a third piece of chocolate cake calls.

Ok, admitted, that's a bit shallow. But I *also* like to look into my eyes, or at my forehead, or at my locked knee. Seeing myself so close in the mirror helps me to settle into my purpose for the class that day; to build a bubble around myself; to meditate.

In his book, The Tibetan Book of Living and Dying, Sogyal Rinpoche tells us that meditation has a core purpose,

*...to awaken in us the sky-like nature of the mind, and to introduce us to that which we really are, our unchanging pure awareness, which underlies the whole of life and death.*

With such an eloquent description as our usual frame of reference, I think most of us associate meditation with contemplative thinking while sitting cross-legged on a comfortable pillow, candles flickering, jasmine incense burning, and perhaps—just to seal the ambience deal— some gentle New Age music playing (here I'm thinking of a concert harp in duet with the mating call of a humpback whale).

Bikram says if that's your cup of tea, fine, but as far as he's concerned all you're going to get from that kind of meditation is "...a fat ass and a lazy body." He instead urges us to practice his Sequence, which Bikram calls one long, hot meditation:

*We put incredible pressure on you to teach you to break your attachment to external things and go within. ... You've got to face yourself in the mirror, every part you don't like, every mistake you make, every excuse your mind creates to limit your potential liberation—there's no place to run, nowhere to hide. No escape from reality... That's why I say that the darkest place in the world is under the brightest lamp. In the Torture Chamber of my class, you will find a beautiful light, and the source of that light is within you.*

Of these two types of meditation, I think I most strongly resonate with Bikram's vision: that the best way I can learn to meditate is by getting my butt kicked, staying silent and still, realizing that I have the strength within me to overcome the physical adversities and mental trials of class. It is that same strength that you and I must rely on to overcome the challenges, pains, and fears we face every day.

I wasn't thinking a lick about any of that—well maybe the fat ass and lazy body part, but definitely not the rest—during class on Week 3/Day 16 of my Challenge. The only thoughts in my head were about Kate, who had been hurting for a week and was terribly sick that day. I had only come to yoga because our friend Jennifer said she would go on a walk with Kate while I was in class.

At that moment we were part way through the 90 minutes and I was concentrating on Standing Separate Leg Stretching pose, wondering just when I had developed two stiff strands of unyielding wire cable for hamstrings.

I was supposed to raise my arms overhead with palms together, then take a four-foot step to the right while simultaneously dropping my arms to parallel to the floor, all the while looking in the mirror to make sure my alignment remained true. No problem; so far so good. But then, after pigeon-toeing my feet in, Chris tells us to bend forward and reach down to grab our feet from the outside, both hands under our heels, *with our legs locked straight at the knees*. I can't even reach my heels so for the hundredth time I settle for grabbing my ankles.

Chris moves on, "Pull hard on our heels; roll forward on your toes until your forehead touches the floor. If you can get there, your goal is to have your forehead touching right between your feet."

Sorry, Chris, I'm still a couple of instructions back trying to lock my legs.

So I try to straighten my legs, grimacing, my hamstrings again fighting me. As I struggle I momentarily reflect that my stretching woes can't be genetic. Into her 70s my Mom can touch the flat of her palms against the ground while bending over with dead straight legs, something she likes to remind me of *at least* four or five times a year.

I continue to pull the wires taut, then pull some more and finally feel a bit of give and wonder if just maybe I'm a bit further along than last week. I smile at the thought, remembering to try to be happy in small things... sometimes *really* small things.

Triangle follows, the Master Pose, the one that everyone seems a bit scared of as it can be truly physically daunting. While I claim no mastery of the pose, for some reason Triangle never puts me in a funk. Maybe it's because instructors often say, "We've reached the half way point of class. It's all downhill from here." So I get a momentary sense of giddiness that I may make it through another class without passing out. At least that thought always used to work for me until I realized Triangle is only the ninth of 26 poses. Whose math makes that half way?

We start the pose looking in the mirror again. Chris tells us to raise our hands overhead with palms together, then to take a four-foot step to the right with arms dropping simultaneously so they parallel the floor, palms down. From there, still looking at ourselves, we pivot our feet, the right one out $90°$, the left $45°$. Next we bend our right knees until our thighs are parallel to the floor, spine straight, hips, body, arms, and face still facing the mirror, all in alignment (OK, I'm starting to think, maybe this isn't so easy...).

"Now turning both palms forward," Chris says, "move only your arms keeping the spine straight, torso stable. Reach down with the right arm and up with the left, placing the right elbow in front of the knee and putting your fingertips to the floor between  the big toe and second toe. No weight on your fingertips! Turn your head up to touch the shoulder so that the profile of your face is visible in the mirror. Arms stretching simultaneously in opposite directions like a human tug of war. Now breathe and hold...(time passes)...freeze in the pose...(more time passes)...and release."

Then we go to the left side. And there's a second set on each side, as well.

I think the title "Master Pose" is well deserved. From a physical standpoint, Bikram claims that Triangle addresses every gland, organ, and system in the body and thus may be the most therapeutic of all the *asanas*. Surely I feel a sense of renewal each time I complete the pose.

Sogyal Rinpoche speaks of the gift of the renewal and realization—here in the guise of a gift from the master—in this way:

> *Imagine the nature of mind as your own face; it is always with you, but you cannot see it without help. Now imagine that you have never seen a mirror before. The introduction by the master is like holding up a mirror suddenly in which you can, for the first time, see your own face reflected. Just like your face, this pure awareness ... is not something "new" that the master is giving you which you did not have*

*before…It has always been yours, and has always been with you, but up until that startling moment you have never actually seen it directly.*

So it is that in yoga a simple idea like looking at yourself in the mirror can, in the blink of an eye, transform into a revelation about the very essence of your being.

With Triangle out of the way, it's supposed to be "all downhill from here", right? If that's true, I want to know how Standing Separate Leg to Knee pose fits in? Over the years this pose has grown to be my nemesis. The setup is a bit like Triangle: arms together overhead, thumbs crossed, arms locked; take a three-foot step to the right (arms still up). This time again pivot the feet 90° and 45° but at the same time turn your hips and torso to the right.

"Turn your hips one, two, three times to bring them in line," Chris tells the class. "Now keeping both your legs straight, stretch up to the ceiling then look at your stomach and curl your body up, out, and then down, bringing your forehead to your knee, arms perfectly straight, hands in prayer position in front of your toes." The posture is said to compress the thyroid gland and thus be good for controlling metabolism and the immune system. Mostly I feel the compression as a choking off of my throat. I can't breathe!

Nor can I get my knees to straighten but Chris comes to my rescue saying, "If you can't get your front leg straight then bend your knee as much as you need to get forehead to knee contact."

Whew…but then I try to follow his words and even that doesn't help. I struggle some more, heat pouring out

from the ceiling fan above me,
sweat dripping off my chin. And the
struggle gets worse; because of my
inverted position the dripping sweat
lands directly in my nostrils, causing
them to burn.

Drip, drip, drip.

Since I'm trying to be disciplined I do nothing about
my nose and instead keep trying to touch my head to my
knee. After much concerted effort they still won't touch.
And with my throat choked I still can't breathe. Not that it
matters. Drop after drop of hot, salty sweat continues to
fall from my chin into my nostrils, which by now are full
and incapable of drawing a breath anyway.

Chris is standing by me just then, walking the room,
not giving me a direct correction this time as instructors
often do but talking to everyone. Still I feel his words hot
and close, and I am sure they are for me. "You *must* touch
your head to your knee to get the full benefit. If you don't,
your pose hasn't even started. Remember what Bikram
says, 99% right is still 100% wrong. You *must* touch your
head to your knee—otherwise you're just hanging out
upside down in a hot room with a lot of sweaty people."

The phone at the front desk rings during the
second to the last posture that day. That's a
pretty unusual occurrence, enough so that when a couple
minutes later a second muffled ringing sounds Chris says,
"Wow, somebody really wants to get through. Let's hope
it's not Bikram calling!"

I have my own worry as we work our way through the final breathing, that perhaps something has happened to Kate.   When Chris releases us for final *Savasana* I don't stay, but instead head out the door directly on his heels. The phone rings a third time.  Chris answers and as he talks he looks up at me, nodding his head, and eventually concludes with, "He's standing here beside me.  I'll tell him right now."

"That was Jennifer," Chris says, hanging up.  "Kate's at the emergency room.  She's apparently in great pain."

I turn white and Chris says, "Breathe, my friend.  First just breathe...slow...deep...breathe...   Now is there anything I can do?  Can I drive you to the hospital?"

K ate had been in and out of the hospital a half dozen times in six months, all associated with kidney difficulties resulting from rigorous radiation treatments from recurrent cancer 13 years earlier.  The most recent hospital stay had come unexpectedly at Oregon Health & Science University in Portland, where her long-time oncologist had helped us arrange appointments with a nephrologist and a surgical urologist.  Kate felt so miserable that the nephrologist decided to admit her before even completing the planned office visit.  Over the next few days of tests and consultations with the urologist, Sia Daneshmand, we began to accept that surgery was the only viable option to bring Kate's kidney function back to normal, and to end this on-going cycle of pain and hospitalization.

That surgery decision, interestingly, led to another

decision:   that I should attempt the Bikram Challenge. Yoga uniquely provides a marriage of body, mind, and spirit.  It is one of the few places other than in the depths of the natural world that I can completely lose myself and forget the worries of my day.

Knowing that, Kate was my biggest cheerleader for tackling the Challenge. "It will help you get rid of stress," she told me back then, two months earlier, "give you something to look forward to while I recover, and allow you to feel like you've accomplished something while we're in Oregon for my surgery."

I only knew that the better I felt, the better I would be able to take care of her.

We needed to stay in Oregon for a month for both surgery and complete recovery for Kate.  Thus roughly a month of my 60-day Challenge would need to be accomplished away from Bozeman.  But as I arrived at the emergency room of Bozeman Deaconess Hospital that night after class, the Challenge was the last thing on my mind.  I wondered if we would even be lucky enough to make it to Portland for Kate's scheduled surgery.

I found Kate reeling in pain.   Jennifer looked distraught, and I could tell she had been crying.  Later she told me that it was the first time she really realized just what kind of agony Kate has had to endure over the years.

By the time Jennifer left, I felt upset but also blessed to learn that Kate's Bozeman urologist, Bruce Robertson, had been calling in regularly to check on her progress even as he was returning to Bozeman from clinic duty 120 miles away.  He and his staff had been instrumental to Kate's well being in the past year, and we were grateful for their presence. Dr. Robertson showed up as soon as he returned to town and that night, as so many other times he cared for Kate like she was one of his own family.

The upcoming surgery in Portland, assuming that we made it there, would be Kate's seventh major operation, on top of a dozen other procedures that required anesthesia, hundreds of tests, X-rays, CTs, plus chemotherapy and internal and external radiation extending 14 years back. Yet always, always, always, she pops back up, smiling, not yielding to pain, giving everything she has, walking across the country, being a wife and confidant and best friend, returning with great success to her professional life—damn it, just trying to live the normal life so many of us take for granted.

I am reminded of one particularly hot, humid day at yoga when time and time again folks across the studio fell unceremoniously out of Standing Bow pose. You could sense the collective frustration in the room growing. Watching the melee, Meg, a visiting instructor, said calmly, "Just remember, your practice is not about how many times you fall out of the pose, but about how many times you get back in."

By that definition I was married to the most phenomenal yogini on Earth.

O ur friend Mike called to check on Kate late one night while she was in the Bozeman hospital. Kate was asleep so I stepped out into the hall to talk. I could look down to the room where Kate and I had sat with

Mike, Amelia, and their son Tim while Amelia struggled
with the late stages of cancer. Kate and Amelia had become
friends and confidants years back. Kate's cancer was (and
is) gone; we would never know Amelia cancer-free.

Mike had been a rock, as had Tim, through Amelia's
years of struggling. He was a truly selfless, loving care
giver, no more so than during her last year. As I hung up
from Mike's call I looked down the empty hospital corridor
toward the hospice room where we last saw Amelia. Tears
filled my eyes and my vision clouded over. I had stepped
between the two mirrors, and instead of looking off into
forever, I was staring back at myself.

The me I saw was from 18 months earlier, during Kate
and my spring healing trip to Nova Scotia. For days we
walked the province's remarkable shorelines, watching the
pounding waves, pulling our hoods tight against the fresh
wind. With Kate's past health woes, more recently those
of my father's, and at that moment Amelia struggling back
in Bozeman, I spent much time during those walks
considering life's dualities: yang and yin, ebb and flow,
health and sickness, life and death.

During our absence Amelia took a turn for the worse.
While Kate and I walked along a secluded beach in Nova
Scotia, Amelia had entered the hospital for the last time.
The cancer had spread and fully controlled her body. We
thought often of Amelia, prayed for her for healing or even
just an end to her pain.

Kate and I stayed at a cabin that sat on a lonely
peninsula, the Bay of Fundy to the front, a large estuary to
the back, with a small stream course connecting the two.

The estuary was intermittently empty to expansive mud flats and then filled to the size of a giant lake. Only a tall, thin spit of sand and the stream course separated the estuary lagoon from the Bay of Fundy. The ebb and flow between bay and estuary were stunning. Nowhere on Earth is the tidal bore so ferocious—in places a 30-foot change that could set up raging rapids.

I visited Amelia in the hospital soon after our return to Bozeman from Nova Scotia. She was struggling, great pain in her abdomen and bones, her mind confused by morphine. I held Amelia's hand as she moved toward sleep, but periodically she shook in fits and spasms. Even when she seemed asleep, Amelia would mutter nonsensical words about childhood and flowers and distant relations. Once she squeezed my hand maniacally, and I thought she was passing into death just then, but in another moment she opened her eyes again.

When I left Amelia that day, I headed directly for yoga. I hunkered down into the corner of the studio, the place where the room has an interesting jog, shaping it like a boot heel. The boot heel provides room for just one person. The mirror is close, the heater directly overhead. It feels like a private practice area within the studio, even with 25 people in class. On days I have something troubling—as on this day—I often come early and chose that private spot to roll out my mat and towel.

When class got underway I tried to let go, tried to release all concerns for my friend. Be present. Set outside worries aside. Connect the mind and body. As the class completed the early poses and sweat began to flow, my mind lightened, but thoughts of Amelia never fell far aside.

The front mirrors allow students to scrutinize their postures, yes, but also to search deeply into their eyes and thus their souls. I remember that when I started Bikram's the idea of using the mirror to look into the soul seemed somewhat melodramatic, but over the years I've heard enough muffled sobs to know others come here in part for mental release, and possibly to face the things that frighten them, just as I often do.

When the instructor had us step to the side of our towels for Triangle pose, I looked up to see myself at the edge of the boot heel mirror. Half of my body was reflected in the mirror just 3 feet in front of me; half was reflected in the mirror in the front of the room 15 feet away.

The duality momentarily shocked me, "Is that me in the distance, or the one so close by?" And then I saw that with a slight movement of my body to the right or the left I could shift from one plane to the other, almost effortlessly.

My throat suddenly choked and I found it hard to breathe. How simple, I thought, for me to move from one level of existence to another. Yang and yin, ebb and flow, health and sickness, life and death. Yet how hard the struggle seemed to be for Amelia to pass on....

But was it really hard, or was it simply hard to watch her make the transition? Could her changeover be as simple as sliding from the mirror so close to the one more distant, or was it more like the violence of the flowing tide in the Bay of Fundy, racing from turbulent waters to a peaceful lagoon?

As yoga class closed that day, I knelt for the final exercise, Breath of Fire. Amelia would die before the next time I came to class, but I could not know that just then. I looked into the mirror, fully alone in the boot heel of the room. The instructor clapped rhythmically and I began to exhale in time.

I looked into the mirror, into my own eyes, and for the moment saw into another time. Kate and I were driving away from the cabin in Nova Scotia. I reached over to hold her hand, then glanced up into the car's rear view mirror. I could see out the back window, out into the previously empty estuary, which now was filled, edge to edge, like a giant calm lake.

For a long time after the end of the final breathing exercise I continued to stare into the mirror. Sweat flowed from my forehead, mixing now with a single tear.

Goodbye Amelia, I thought, we love you.

# Chapter 5

# Seeing the Forest & the Trees

*If you don't know the trees*
*you may be lost in the forest...*

—Siberian Elder

E dges are important. Edges are diverse, taking on characteristics of that which they connect. Edges define the place between what is and what is to come. Edges represent transition. That transition could occur in our lives—think of the moment a child is born. Or, the transition could occur in the world around us—think of the meadow at the edge of deep forest.

From my house I can see the entirety of the Bridger Range, with Mount Baldy towering over the Gallatin Valley. The mountain is forested from its base almost to its barren top; only a few meadows and rock outcroppings interrupt the cloak of green.

To climb Baldy you start hiking at a trailhead at the mountain's base, out in the open. But soon you pass into forest and pine and spruce engulf you. Your world becomes an intimate maze of tree trunks and winding trail close at hand. The mountaintop, your goal for the day, is no longer in sight. Yet the trees also hold intrigue: a gnarled trunk covered by moss, a cool breeze carrying the smell of recent rain, underfoot an endless variety of wildflowers, and in the bush ahead the flash of a fleeing deer.

Along the way, near the crest of one of the foothill summits, you cross out of the forest and into a grassy meadow. Standing at edge of the meadow you can see the top of Mount Baldy again. But like the vision from back in the valley, the trees ahead have taken on a more amorphous form, void of features, a single mass of green rising up the mountainside to the peak. The picture from the edge of the meadow is robbed of detail, surely, yet it is so much bigger, providing a renewed vision of your goal for the day.

Standing at the edge of the meadow, at that point of transition, you have a sense of what is to come. Looking at the forest is no more or no less interesting or informative than looking at the trees. It's just different.

I get the feeling that Bikram is one of those people who can see both the trees and the forest. In relatively short order after arriving in the US, he went from considering the physical merits of how to order individual yoga *asanas* for best effect to envisioning and laying the groundwork for a worldwide yoga empire. Now, some four decades later, that business empire has grown so large and dominant that when the CBS show *60 Minutes* did a segment on Bikram, they titled it simply "McYoga".

Bikram blames the commercial aspects of his empire on the actress Shirley MacLaine whom, according to Bikram, he met when she came to India in search of the true meaning of life. In Los Angeles, Bikram did not initially charge for his yoga classes until MacLaine told him that in the States people would not respect him if he did not charge money. So Ms. MacLaine hired a secretary, Jackie, for Bikram and as he says,

> *If you wanted to take my class, you had to pay Jackie three dollars. So Shirley started it. Don't blame me. I arrived in America as a holy, spiritual, innocent, virginal yogi. Why are you laughing? It's true!*

Eventually Bikram even settled on an all American route, franchising, to achieve his goal of bringing yoga to the West. Hence McYoga was born. When asked by the *60 Minutes* interviewer if he liked his studios being referred to as "The McDonalds of Yoga", Bikram replied,

> *Why not? What's wrong with that? I eat Big Mac.*

Bikram did not stop the Americanization of his yoga Sequence at the franchising effort alone. To carve out a piece of the yoga pie that he alone could control, Bikram sought and received federal copyright protection for his yoga Sequence. But how, you might ask, can someone copyright yoga postures that have existed for thousands of years? At different places and times Bikram—in his hurried, sometimes fragmented English—has said,

> *Yoga is free. It belongs to the Earth. It's a God. But I picked up a piece of it and I created something. ... I believed there was a beautiful song that the body could sing to the soul, so I attempted to write it. That song, as I heard it, is the Sequence. ... When Quincy Jones my student takes same do re mi fa, create a melody, become a song, you can copyright that song. So I picked up 26 postures and put in a Sequence like a melody. I created that! ... This is my personal property. It works. You want to do it, you do the right way.*

Bikram's copyright means that to teach the Sequence instructors must go through his training and use his exact Dialogue. According to the *LA Times*, he derives $3 million annually from training the teachers of his Sequence. From a business standpoint Bikram has wrapped his yoga offering in silk and tied it with a tight bow; he has created a true yoga juggernaut.

**W**eek 4/Day 20 of my 60-day Challenge. I am standing, dripping, staring directly into the mirror and listening to Chris say, "The path of yoga is the path of fearlessness." It is a good time for me to hear these words because we are in the last poses, Tree and Toe, of the Standing Series and fear *precisely* describes what I see directly ahead. Why? Because Toe Stand provides a tremendous challenge to the knees.

While I am looking into the mirror, my mind is in another place. I am picturing my left knee, the one that I blew out while skiing at Red Lodge Mountain in seventh grade; the knee that sent me into surgery and a week-long hospital stay; the knee I hobbled along with for another three weeks in a cast. It's the very same knee attached to the ankle that my loving Mother dropped a 15-pound sack of weights on while I was trying to do my home physical therapy routine! Never mind that my stiff knee was hanging over a thin headboard and the falling weights caused it to suddenly accordion and make a sickening crunch, leaving me screaming in pain! Never mind to this day my Mom always reminds me that in retrospect the dropped weights probably are the reason I got my flexibility back and can even walk! Never mind that....

Ok, sorry, I think you get it—I'm a little bit sensitive about my left knee.

Chris again, bringing me back: "Next we do Tree pose, *Tadasana*. Everyone feet together, straight back, hips forward. Shift your weight into the left leg. Reach down and lift up your right foot and place it high on the inside of your thigh."

Possibly sensing my lack of focus, Chris steps off the podium in my direction and says, "Concentrate, meditate, look at yourself in the mirror. Now carefully push your knee down and back, opening the knee and hip joints, standing leg locked, hips in one line, shoulders in one line, both hips and shoulders parallel to the floor and parallel to the mirror."

I look into the mirror and recapture my focus, seeing that my hips and shoulders are canted high-to-low in a way that looks uncomfortable even to me. I shift around but can't make it all

come square.  When I lift one shoulder the opposite hip drops.  And vice versa.

Chris has us raise our right hand up and place it in the center of our chests, hold it, release, and repeat the pose on the opposite side.  Then it's time for Toe Stand.

"Unless you are new here or have had a *recent* knee surgery, say in the last 45 minutes, you should be trying Toe Stand.  This is not an optional pose; this is a beginning Bikram pose.  Remember, if you can you must."

I have never yet tried Toe Stand but in the four weeks of my Challenge I have seen many improvements—perhaps some of them minor but improvements nonetheless—and I have an idea that I just might try Toe today.

Looking down at my left knee in the mirror, I wince.

I think I can best help you understand my knee concerns here by first helping you visualize Toe Stand in its final, full expression.  Start by thinking of a baseball catcher crouched down behind the batter.  The catcher is on the balls of both feet.  Now get rid of the batter and get rid of all that gear: facemask, shin guards, chest protector.  Toss it all.  Heck while you're at it remove a few clothes until the catcher has only his sliding shorts on (since that's all our catcher has on, let's make him a man this time).  Now pull the right leg out from under him and cross the foot over onto the left thigh.  That's correct, our man is now balanced on the ball of the left foot alone, one point of contact between his body and the ground, all his weight being held by the deeply bent left knee.  Now, just to make it a

bit more challenging, let's have him toss the mitt aside and instead put his hands in prayer position in front of his heart…and, oh yea, press up on the toes and hold it there for a while.

Sound tough?  Sure does to me.  And painful for my bad knee.  But now after many weeks, years actually, of just hanging out for a second round of Tree while others try Toe Stand I have decided that today is the day I will try. Today I will push my edge.  I choose to will myself forward because I believe—or at least I really want to believe—one of Bikram's oft repeated maxims:

> It's never too late, it's never too bad, and
> you're never too old or too sick
> to start from scratch once again.

Chris gets us into Toe Stand just like we started Tree: feet together, shifting our weight into the left leg.  "Lift your right foot high onto the left thigh," he says, "then this time bring both hands into prayer position."  I do so and my foot falls pitifully from my thigh to my knee, but I am committed so I just leave the darn thing there.

"Keep your gaze fixed on the floor four feet in front of you," Chris continues.  "Now bend forward from the lower spine, reach down, and touch your fingertips on the floor for support."

It's only been the last few days, after three plus years of yoga, that I've made it to touching my fingertips to the floor.  Understand that this is one step before all that catcher-balanced-on-one-foot nonsense.  My knee and leg quiver dramatically as I just barely get my fingers to the floor. While my leg shakes like Elvis writhing through *Blue Suede Shoes*, Chris tells us to slowly sink down into the squatting position, coccyx on the left heel.

Yikes, this is the catcher part. Trouble is I have never even made it to the squatting position. I try to bend my knee but it continues to quake like Jell-O.

So I stop.

Others are struggling at the same place I'm stuck and Chris urges us to go deeper. "Don't be afraid to try," he says. "You must go to your edge and then beyond. Heck, you might even fall down. But it's ok; we all need to be more like toddlers and not be afraid to fall down."

Bikram's wife Rajashree, a five-time All-India Yoga Champion herself, reportedly once said, "Fear is the biggest challenge we face in yoga." As for me, I *do* realize that I am afraid. Over thirty years after my knee surgery I'm willing to admit that what stops me in Toe Stand is almost surely more mental than physical.

So I recommit myself. I try again to bend my knee and squat down, pushing hard, pushing through my fear, going to a place I've never been before, up to and beyond the edge of my fear and pain....and...and amazingly, my knee actually does bend and I start to go down into the squat and I am so excited and scared and proud and...

...and then quickly and with no grace *whatsoever* I fall to the floor in a loud crash, almost knocking over Cristina, Sandy, Tahnee, Casey, Amy, and Tara like so many dominoes lined up in a row.

Lying on the floor, miscellaneous body parts scattered about me in a pool of sweat, I can sense Chris looking my way and smiling.  I'm convinced he loves to see pain.  "See there, my friend," he says, "that didn't hurt a bit, did it?"

C alling Bikram's yoga empire a "juggernaut", as I did earlier, is actually a pretty good choice of words.   Juggernaut, as we use it, describes a metaphorical or literal force so overwhelming, so unstoppable that it will crush anything in its path.   The word is derived from the Sanskrit *Jaganntha*, which means "Lord of the Universe". The name is synonymous with Krishna, the Hindu deity often represented as a young prince giving philosophical direction, a deity who continues today to have fanatic followers.

With studios opening all over the world, the image of Bikram Yoga as an unstoppable force is evident, and Bikram's storyline might also include some fanatic followers. It makes sense.  Bikram has all the qualities— charm, charisma, singularity of purpose, a promise to help you improve your life if you will only follow him—to make him a leader attractive to jump in line behind.

And some people do jump.  Hilary MacGregor, an *LA Times* staff reporter, attended one of Bikram's teacher training classes at his LA studio.  As MacGregor relates, Bikram enters the studio, walks to the front and "...climbs into a chair perched like a throne..." above the aspiring teachers.   When he asks the class of 300 to introduce themselves, one of the trainees stands and says to the gathered congregation, "I love Bikram.  He is God."

Eeuuww!

So it is that Bikram's business juggernaut may be built,

at least for a few anyway, on a foundation of blind faith. Couple that with copywriting yoga poses that belong to everyone and his cutthroat business tactics and surely this is not...

...Ok, but let's hold here. I think I need to step back for a moment. Why? Because the game of analysis and criticism of the Bikram juggernaut is an easy one and playing it feels like so much piling on. There are many seeming contradictions about Bikram, not the least of which is the apparent hypocrisy between his own posh lifestyle and the philosophy of a simple life he purports to believe in.

But truth is, I don't really care.

I've never had much of a disciple mentality. I'm too much of a critical thinker to accept everything I hear or see at face value. I'm not big on buying words without evidence, even if the speaker is charismatic, as Mr. Bikram Choudhury surely is. It *is* true that the heavy commercial overtones of Bikram Yoga bug me. The commercialism could even offend my egalitarian side enough to send me looking for another place to practice, or another activity to undertake.

But I choose to set all the outside criticisms and my own concerns aside for a measure that is far more tangible: doing Bikram Choudhury's yoga Sequence makes me feel good—physically, mentally, spiritually. I have my own solid evidence that what he teaches is helping me transform into a better person.

For me that's enough.

Maybe other types of yoga would enliven and

invigorate me as well; I don't know, but I do know that this one does. So does Bikram see the forest for the trees? On days when I walk out of class reenergized and rejuvenated I'm forced to wonder if he doesn't also see the mountains the woods grow upon, and the individual needles in the pines.

B aseball catcher Lawrence Peter Berra is probably more famous today as America's definitive source of malapropisms than for his long baseball career. You probably know him better as "Yogi". A friend nicknamed him Yogi because the friend thought Berra looked like a Hindu holy man when he sat cross legged (though I'm guessing not actually *in* Full Lotus pose) while waiting for his turn at bat.

Even without Full Lotus, Berra speaks in the wise ways of a yogi. It was he, for example, who perfectly captured the state of my 60-day Challenge when he said,

*Ninety per cent of the game is mental, the other half is physical.*

My Challenge had indeed rounded almost entirely into a mental game—well except I suppose for the 50% of it that was sore muscles and achy hamstrings. Almost four weeks complete and counting. The half way point to ten weeks loomed just ahead and in this fourth week I felt that I had made an important mental transition: I now believed that physically I had it in me to successfully complete the Challenge.

But true to Mr. Berra's words, I also felt that I had 140% of life on my plate. Why? Yogi again:

*You can observe a lot by watching.*

Anyone observing me after yoga on Week 4/Day 22 would surely have been able to see that I was suffering, and not just from sore muscles. Rebekah had taught class that day and along the way told us, "Suffering is what happens when the mind won't let go of what is." The "what is" we faced was departing Bozeman for Oregon and Kate's surgery. My head spun through a thousand visions of CTs and X-rays, IVs and medications, needles and blood draws, doctors and nurses and hospital beds, and especially, especially worries about Kate being in pain.

I felt stressed; the time had come.

I walked from the studio that day into downtown Bozeman, where I would meet Kate for our final good luck meal on our way out of town. We went to La Tinga's, our favorite restaurant in town. Kurt and Alba, our friends and La Tinga owners, refused to let us pay. It was an act of simple friendship born of their desire to wish us the best in Oregon, and it took me by such surprise that I had to step outside for a moment to clear tears from my eyes.

What *would* happen? We were heading back to the coast for Kate's seventh major surgery and I was finding it impossible to get past the details to see the big picture: that this surgery could make her well again, that this journey could serve as our transition into a new life.

I couldn't see all that. I could only see the words of my personal yogi, Mr. Lawrence Peter Berra, flashing across my mind:

*It's like déjà vu all over again.*

# Chapter 6

# Dead Bodies All In a Row

*If your mind is empty,*
*It is always ready for anything;*
*It is open to everything.*

—Shunryn-Suzuki

J ust an hour out of Bozeman, as we drove west, Kate and I crossed the Continental Divide at Homestake Pass and joined the waters heading for the Pacific. It was a symbolic crossing for us, heralding our return to Oregon where we had lived so many years, where we had discovered and fought with Kate's cancer and then recurrent cancer. This trip was to be a reverse of our U-Haul move to Montana, a move prompted at least in part by our walk across the state along the Continental Divide Trail ten years earlier. Over 800 miles and almost three months backpacking through Montana's wildlands, days filled with health and hope and love.

And now here we were again, looking west off the Divide, thinking of the beauty of all those miles along the crest of the continent—golden sunrises far out over the plains, aqua marine lakes reflecting rugged peaks, herds of elk racing into the forest, alpine meadows dancing with wildflowers—beauty so overwhelming it could cause your heart to swell and eyes to mist over. Walking like that, day after day after day through wild country, brought Kate and me boundless joy.

My throat choked with emotion as we sped across the Divide and all I could think of was *just breathe.* Believe in what we are doing. In the coming weeks we would need to live by the tenets of the old adage[4],

*Life is not measured by the number of breaths we take, but by the moments that take our breath away.*

I knew that to sustain ourselves during the next month in Oregon, we would need to return to memories of past times that took our breath away. For the next month, those memories would have to be how we would measure our lives and occupy our minds.

G eoffrey West, President of and Distinguished Professor at the Santa Fe Institute, postulates that all animals have the same number of heartbeats over the course of their lives. Whales, whose hearts beat roughly 20 times/minute, live a *long* time. Shrews, on the other hand, with a heartbeat of some 1000 times/minute, live but a few years. But when you multiply the heart rate by the length of time lived, according to West, the total

---

[4] An adage which, interestingly enough, I once saw credited to the often acerbic, late comedian George Carlin.

number of heart beats in a lifetime for all animals comes out close to the same number, frighteningly close.

Surprised?    Dr. West was, calling his discovery "astonishing".

But as West continues to explore his model does seem to work—for shrews, rats, lions, elephants. Humans don't *quite* fit the model, but not because the model is faulty. Instead it is because we've cheated the game by inventing things like sanitation and medicine. But the idea is still worth considering. "If these laws are true," West says, "what they're telling you is there is an extraordinary unity to all of life."

Turns out that Dr. West even knows the magic lifetime number, 1.5 billion heartbeats from birth to death, though he is quick to add "roughly". Well yea.

Some Indian religions purport that, as with West's theory of heartbeats, the number of breaths in a lifetime is similarly pre-determined. By that logic if you slow the breath, you live longer. Hmmm... Slowing the breath equals slowing the heart, right? And slowing the heart, given a fixed number of heartbeats in your lifetime, would also mean living longer. Wow, it all fits together!

As for me, I'm approaching the mid-century mark. By conventional thought—let's face it, we all hope to live to be 100—my days are roughly half numbered. Measuring my heart rate just now, as I am sitting and rested, I get 50 beats per minute. Let's run with that. According to West, at 1.5 billion beats for my lifetime I've got 30,000,000 minutes to make my mark on the planet. That equates to

500,000 hours ...or...let's see carry the one...er...20,833 days...or...(gulp)...57.1 years.

What! Fifty-seven years? Now hold on just a doggone minute, that means I have less than ten years to go!

I think I better get to work.

T hough Tree pose and Toe Stand supposedly bring your respiration and heart rates down, more than once I've arrived at that point in Bikram's class, the completion of the Standing Series, with lungs sucking for air and heart racing. I always reach this point hot and sweaty, frequently find my skin sizzling and feverish, and sometimes even feel woozy and ready to fall to the floor. Thankfully Bikram chose to end the standing portion of the Sequence right here and send his students into *Savasana*.

*Savasana* is the Dead Body Pose, a posture of deep relaxation. Bikram claims that *Savasana* is the most important posture in yoga. I can go with that. And why not? Who could be against slovenly repose?

Outwardly *Savasana* surely seems to be the easiest pose in the Sequence. You simply lie flat on your back, relaxed, arms and legs straight, hands close to your body with palms facing upward, heels touching with feet falling open. Eyes should be open, perhaps focused softly on a point on the ceiling, to help you stay present in the room and in the moment. Now remain perfectly still, breathe normally, and relax...be the dead body.

Simple, right?

Well sort of. The problem with *Savasana* is that the mind wants

to wander, even when you think you are "doing it right".
When I stare at the ceiling I try to get my eyes to glaze
over—still open, but unfocused.  More and more often
these days I'm successful at stopping my mind from racing
about through today's worries or tomorrow's schedule, but
I can't seem to master the art of softening my eyes.  I try to
look up blankly, but have found that the cuts and dents in
the ceiling boards hold boundless treasures:  once I could
see the lines in the gypsum meld into the form of a sphinx,
another time into the constellation Orion, still another
time into a Cheshire cat.

Whether it be the wandering mind for many, or the
eyes as an extension of the mind for me, the difficulty in
*Savasana* derives from our inability to let go and *simply be*.
Bikram says that relinquishing control terrifies the mind.
He calls the mind rebellious, with an agenda of its own.
Izumi Shikibu, a Japanese poet who lived around 1000 AD,
describes the mind's rebellious nature this way:

> *Although I try to hold the single thought*
> *of Buddha's teaching in my heart,*
> *I cannot help but hear the many crickets' voices*
> *calling as well.*

A wandering cricket's voice calls to me just now.
Surely *Savasana* is, at its core, meditation.  I know that
you're not supposed to lie down during "true"
meditation—I'm guessing the thought is that some of us
might just doze off—but still there is much here that is
same.  I mean what is meditation after all?  Dr. Joan
Borysenko, a pioneer in the field of mind/body medicine,

says that meditation can be broadly defined as any activity that keeps one's attention pleasantly anchored in the present moment.  Sure sounds like *Savasana* to me.

But I like Sogyal Rinpoche's metaphor about meditation, and by extension about the purpose of *Savasana*, even better:

> *I often compare the mind in meditation to a jar of muddy water. The more we leave the water without interfering or stirring it, the more the particles of dirt will sink to the bottom, letting the natural clarity of the water shine through. The very nature of the mind is such that if you only leave it in its unaltered and natural state, it will find its true nature, which is bliss and clarity.*

I'm guessing that Bikram, who says that meditation is the practice of focusing and calming the mind, would like Sogyal Rinpoche's metaphor.  "My job," Bikram has written, "is to help you prepare your body, which will quiet the mind, and begin to build a solid foundation for a Spiritual life."

Time and time again my teachers have echoed Bikram's belief that the most important posture for preparation of the body and quieting of the mind is *Savasana*.  There is almost a reverence for the pose.  Many instructors say it is the hardest pose we do.  One instructor even went so far as to say that if you can master it, *Savasana* is the only yoga you will ever need.

Mastering *Savasana* seems like it shouldn't be that tough.  We simply need to learn to get out of our own way.

U nable to sleep at our hotel room in Coeur d'Alene, thinking about the drive the next day to Portland, I tried to slip into *Savasana*, one of the few poses of the Sequence that Bikram and his instructors encourage you to enter anytime, anywhere. I positioned myself gingerly, trying not to wake Kate. Then I lay quietly for a long time, staring at the bumps on the darkened ceiling, remembering.

While we rested in *Savasana* one day, Chris asked us to consider how that in death we are for the first time released from pain and suffering, how in death we are for the first time truly at peace. (How anyone is supposed to keep a clear mind with that kind of stirring of the mud befuddles me.... But I digress.)

"Why is it," Chris asked further, "that we have to wait until death to achieve that wonderful state of peace and ease when instead we can experience it right here on Earth, in *Savasana*, the Dead Body pose?"

Staring up at the darkened ceiling, it dawned on me that practicing *Savasana* could be thought of as practicing for death.


I like the idea of mind control. The kind of mind control I'm talking about is having the power to shut down your inner thoughts to the extent that the mind becomes just another body part, like the leg or the liver. In this line of thinking the mind is not you, then, but instead something that you can control. Bikram covers it this way, saying,

*Without control of the mind, you can do*
*nothing...Nobody knows how much power they truly*
*possess—how much heart power, physical power, mental*
*power, spiritual power—until they can train their mind to a*
*point at which they can silence all the unnecessary*
*chatter...The greatest challenge we face as human beings is*
*controlling and properly using our own minds.*

So if the mind is not you, who takes control and tells your mind to "just hush up"? The answer—depending on who you are listening to—is the Self or, equivalently, the Soul or the Spirit. Bikram puts the mind in an intermediary place, saying that it acts as the communications system between the physical body and the Self/Soul/Spirit.

Seeing the Self/Soul/Spirit as something that exists on a plane above and beyond the mind is a hard concept, no doubt. But if it's true, then it seems reasonable that the mind *could* be controlled by the Self/Soul/Spirit. If so, suddenly the crickets can be silenced and *Savasana* becomes possible.

As he was nearing death from cancer, runner and cardiologist George Sheehan came to some deep insights regarding the human condition. In Going the Distance he recorded his thoughts about the very same Self or Soul or Spirit we've been talking about (though Sheehan chose not to capitalize them):

*My self is not my body, although for most of my life I*
*thought so; did I not have control of my body? Epictetus,*
*who defined the self as what we could control, said no. And*
*once disease and age set in, I recognized that truth. I can get*
*the most out of my body. I can be an athlete. But the*

*athlete I am and the maximum performance I can attain is my body's domain, and not mine.*

It's clear that in his final days Sheehan came to the conclusion that the body is not the Self. That realization must have been a difficult one, especially for a longtime athlete and runner, as it appears to have come at the point when he could no longer control his physical person.

I have not yet experienced the transition Sheehan speaks of, the realization that the body exists in a domain separate from the Spirit. My Father saw it. His Parkinson's and arthritis took away his ability to use his hands normally. My Dad was a former all-star college basketball player and once when he awkwardly held a basketball it about broke my heart. "I just can't feel the ball," he said. "It's like we used to say about having 'no touch'. I don't have any touch."

Just as it was not his body, Sheehan realized that his Self/Soul/Spirit was also not his mind:

*My self is not my mind, either. Although for most of my life I thought so. As a physician and a writer I depended on my mental skills. As they diminished I saw my self diminishing with them.*

Importantly Dr. Sheehan eventually found hope. He realized that it was not inevitable, even while suffering from terminal cancer, that all parts of his being would deteriorate:

*...the general rule is for the body-mind machine to decline. What does not decline is the soul. The soul is forever young,*

*forever growing, forever gaining new powers and new insights. True, it must use the body and the mind to gain these powers. The values and the virtues forever in the process are gained through the body and the mind. Until they fail completely, my self, which is my soul, will continue to grow.... Each of us has a body-mind instrument, however flawed, through which we can make our soul. That is the secret of life.*

As Sheehan was moving toward his ultimate act on Earth, death, it seems clear that he had grown to see the Soul, the Self, the Spirit, as existing separate from his mind and body. We can only hope that in death he found the peace and ease that Chris once spoke of as available in Dead Body pose.

# Chapter 7

# Changing Winds

*The pessimist complains about the wind;*
*The optimist expects it to change;*
*And the realist adjusts the sails.*

-William Arthur Ward

O ne day in the mid-90s, Kate and I found ourselves paddling north along the exposed eastern shore of Isla Carmen. Isla Carmen sits part way between Mulege and La Paz, Mexico, roughly three miles off the shore of Baja California. The Sea of Cortez here is famous for its heavy winds that drive out of the north, paralleling the Baja Peninsula unimpeded for hundreds of miles and creating massive seas. Sea kayakers call the wind simply El Norte. El Norte has ruined many a kayaking trip, and in a few instances killed people.

We had been battling El Norte for a couple hours, paddling directly into its gaping maw, making almost no progress. For every two strokes we took forward El Norte drove us one stroke backwards. Far ahead—because of their superior paddling and not because they started earlier than us—we could see our friends Jeff and Linda turn in toward a small headland. Like us they paddled close to shore, hoping against hope to find any possible relief from the wind.

By the time we came abreast of them we found Jeff and Linda pulled out onto a rocky beach. They had spotted a tiny, sheltered cove, protected by the narrow, jutting headland. Cliffs separated the beach from the dry interior of the island. Jeff and Linda helped us land and then we all sat down to assess the situation.

Twenty yards off shore the wind continued in its frenzied rush south. We could hear the howling, but for the moment we felt great relief for our protected, albeit tenuous, position. Big rollers, pushed by the gale, stacked up on each other one after another, heading passed us as if the waters were part of some giant, flowing river of rapids. El Norte blew the crests off the waves, the frothing white tops contrasting with the deep blue of the sea to make for a scene that was chaotic and frightening, yet also surreal and sublimely beautiful. Far in the distance, back in the direction we came, we could see the waves pile-drive into the rocky shore of a bay that lie just inside an easterly projecting isthmus. Both the bay and the isthmus had been relatively calm when we paddled by them earlier.

After silently taking it all in, a quick pow-wow brought the four of us to a decision.

"Good god it's harsh out there. Look at those waves!"

"I don't think I could have gone on a hundred yards farther. My arms and back are killing me. I think we gotta stop."

"Yea, me too. I don't think I can take anymore of Hell Norte today."

"Me, neither."

"But hold on a sec. It's only just past lunch. If we stop it's going to be hard to make it around the island in the days we have left. We'll have to go back."

"True, but if we go ahead this afternoon we die. So take your choice."

"Ok, I know, I know."

"Hey, we got plenty of food and water, right? But do we still have tequila?"

"*We* do, how about you?"

"No, but *we* have fresh limes."

"Will you share?"

"Will you?"

Nods around. "OK, then it's settled, we stay."

"Agreed, we stay."

So it was a unanimous decision, driven by the wind and built on a foundation of tequila and limes: sit tight and camp on the protected, rocky shore.

Later, warmed by an afternoon of contemplation, we decided to rise early and try to get out before El Norte showed the next day. In our experience to that moment, if El Norte was going to arrive it most often started to whip up around noon, but on the odd day it might start earlier, even by breakfast. We decided not to take any chances and instead try to push off at sunup.

By 5 AM the next morning we had packed and eaten. A glimmer of orange showed to the east as we readied our kayaks at shore's edge. Try as we might, we could see no

details of the sea outside our protected cove, but we could
hear the wind still howling.

"I *think* it's quieter than last night, don't you?" ...
"Yea, maybe, I guess so" ... "Sure the wind still seems to
be up but it *couldn't* be as bad as yesterday, right?" ... "No
way, couldn't be as bad." ... "I say we go." ... "Ok, let's
go!" So at the first hint of light we stowed our headlamps
and pushed off.

It was worse.

Twenty yards out the wind rudely wrestled the boats
from our control and turned them south. In a breath we
were too far from shore in too big of waves to even
consider trying to turn around across the wind and waves
and head back for dry land. We began to bob up and
down, the waves lifting us and dropping us like a cheap fair
ride. Within 30 seconds we lost any chance to yell back
and forth between the boats. Suddenly we were surfing
down waves, trying to keep from broaching and dumping
into the sea. Jeff and Linda paddled ahead, clearly fighting
the sea themselves. We tried to stay close, following their
silhouette backed by the faint glow now rising from below
the horizon.

As the sun poked up and we could make out what lie
ahead, it quickly became apparent to Kate and me that the
waves were carrying us directly back toward the rocky bay.
Even clearer came the realization that we would be
smashed to smithereens if we did not paddle *farther out* to
sea to make it around the rocky isthmus we had come
around the previous morning. The recognition of our
predicament brought up a major challenge: to get farther

out to sea we had to paddle sideways to the wind and waves, a precarious position ripe for dumping. But we had no choice.

We could see ahead that Jeff and Linda had come to the same realization. We tried to follow them as closely as possible in case one of the boats dumped. At least I should say tried to follow them *when* we could see them. Each boat had 12-foot sailing masts—sails currently stowed—and as Jeff and Linda went down into the wave troughs the top of their mast disappeared. We only saw them when we both hit the wave crests at the same time. Up and down we bobbed, paddling out to sea, Kate and me screaming to each other that the next wave was coming and bringing the kayak back into line, fighting with paddle and rudder against broaching, fighting not to dump as we surfed down the wave, taking a breath, and then repeating the cycle.

For two and a half hours.

For a time Jeff and Linda pulled far ahead, but strangely by the time we finally made it to the outside of the isthmus we arrived almost together. Unbeknownst to us, somewhere out in the giant waves Jeff had yelled over the wind, "Quit paddling so hard, Linda, we might as well all die together."

We finally crossed behind the isthmus and found a protected beach out of the wind and waves. Pulling into the beach we all staggered out of the boats. 8:15 AM. For a moment no one said anything. We dropped onto the beach and stared out to sea, white lipped, dumbfounded, looking out beyond the protection of the isthmus, out to where the wind raged on.

Finally someone spoke, "I think that's the stupidest thing I've ever done in my life."

"Me too."

"Yea, me too."

Then someone else, "That's it. I'm done for the day. No more Hell Norte for me."

"Me neither."

"Me neither."

"Agreed."

After a day of sunshine and collapse we paddled on the following morning. By late afternoon we found ourselves camped along a beautiful inlet, now on the south side of Isla Carmen and out of reach of El Norte. We read, we snorkeled, we hiked into the island's interior, Jeff caught a mackerel and we barbequed it, we saw a fin whale remarkably near to shore, a pod of dolphins come into our inlet and entertained us for an hour. Worries of the past days' trials by El Norte fell away.

Early that evening we sat on the beach, four happy friends glowing with the heat of the sun and happy memories of the day's events. We looked out beyond the mountains of the mainland to an orange sunset that grew from the west, then arched across the sky transforming to scarlet, then red, then pink and finally in the East to the coming purple of twilight where the night's first stars twinkled. So startling was the beauty that no one spoke. Nowhere could such an incredible sunset occur but in Baja.

We sipped on our tequila, content with the serenity of the moment, content to watch the scene unfold before us, until someone said, "You know, we have to cross a big opening over to the other island tomorrow. So there'll be plenty of exposure if El Norte comes up again."

Not to worry, came the response from one, and soon we all four agreed. We sat silently for a time again, thinking our own thoughts. This moment, just now, was special and needed to be enjoyed. We could not know if El Norte would return the following day. As a group we had learned the words of Koji, a character in Japanese literature, who said,

*Tomorrow's wind blows tomorrow.*

That would be our philosophy for the rest of the journey.

K ate and I pushed into the wind in eastern Washington and then through the Columbia Gorge as we made our way to Corvallis Oregon, where we would stay for a few days before checking her into the hospital in Portland. Upon arrival in Corvallis, we quickly beat a path to my sister Suz's house. Suz and her husband Dennis and daughters Brittney and Jordan welcomed us for a few days rest before our time at the Portland hospital. It felt good that even though we were so far away from Montana, with such a stressful time at hand, that we could also feel so at home and comfortable among loving family.

Once settled at Suz and Dennis's, it did not take me long to find my way to the local Bikram studio on the south end of town. I had to get there; the Challenge required me to do yoga six days of every seven, and the drive day from Idaho counted as my day off for the week.

I had never attended another Bikram's studio beyond

Chris and Rebekah's, but in short order I felt welcome. I soon met Elizabeth, the kind owner in Corvallis, along with a couple of her instructors, Steve and Jeanie, and they all provided their sincere best wishes for Kate, not to mention encouragement to me for my Challenge.

The power of the franchise became evident when I stepped into the Corvallis studio. Lying on my mat, waiting for class to start, the heat settled over me like a warm blanket. I felt at home. I began to revel in the realization that just as in Chris and Rebekah's studio, I had come to a safe place, to a place where I might gather strength to cope with the troubles of the world. When Elizabeth entered the room and asked us to stand up on our mats, clasp our hands, and begin *Pranayama* breathing, I felt an immediate sense of community with the 30 people standing around me. Inhaling deeply, I realized that I had not come that day in search of a new form of yoga, but instead felt happy to see the same series of poses I already knew unfold before me.

The number of forms of yoga seems to be a matter of much debate. As a fledgling student of yoga with a true beginner's inquisitiveness, I searched to find how many forms of yoga exist. I quickly learned that not only is there no agreement on how many forms of yoga there are, folks can't even seem to agree on what to call the multiple forms.

The Bhagavad Gita emphasizes just *three* forms of yoga: Karma, Bhakti, and Jnana. Shine on Yoga lists *four* main "branches" of yoga—Karma, Bhakti, Jnana, and Raja—

though they do hasten to add that Hatha yoga and Kundalini yoga are"sub-paths" of Raja yoga. By contrast, *self-realization.com* says that there are *six* yoga "systems" and the Yoga School of Kailua lists *seventeen* "kinds" of yoga.[5] While Bikram Yoga is named as one of the seventeen yogas, the Yoga School of Kailua describes Bikram Yoga in a straightforward but seemingly dismissive fashion as a "currently very popular fad yoga". Interestingly, the same web page shows a gorgeous, shapely, bikini-clad woman doing yoga on a tropical beach. Neither "sand yoga" nor "bikini yoga" is one of their seventeen kinds of yoga listed.

Top prize for the number of forms of yoga, at least in my survey, goes to *Yoga Journal*. They call yoga a "philosophy" and describe *20* yoga "disciplines".[6] Like the Yoga School of Kailua, *Yoga Journal* labels Bikram's as one of the disciplines of yoga.

It's odd that several sources label Bikram Yoga as a form, branch, system, kind, or discipline of yoga since Mr. Bikram Choudhury, who has on occasion been described as an egotist, does not.

W eek 5/Day 25 and 26. For the first time I planned to take two classes in a single day. It

---

[5] The seventeen are Abhava, Adhyatma, Ast-anga, Bhakti, Bikram, Classic, Gnana, Hatha, Integral, Iyengar, Jnana, Karma, Kriya, Kundalina (also known as Laya), Mantra, Power, and Raja.

[6] The 20 are Ananda, Anusara, Ashtanga, Bikram, Hatha, Integral, Integrative Yoga Therapy, ISHTA, Iyengar, Jivamukti, Kripalu, Kundalini, Phoenix Rising Yoga Therapy, Power Yoga, Sivananda, Svaroopa, Tibetan, TriYoga, Viniyoga, and White Lotus.

was a Sunday, the day before we would take Kate to the hospital in Portland. Not knowing what awaited us, I decided that if I could get two of my six days completed for the week, the odds increased that I might not have to quit my Challenge during Kate's hospital time.

Lying in Dead Body Pose at the completion my second Standing Series of the day, I realized that having made it this far I probably I could make it through two classes in a single day without fear of collapse. I also drew strength from knowing that the yoga was helping relieve the stress of worrying about the week ahead. I needed just then to draw on our lesson learned years earlier at the hands of El Norte, the same lesson that Buddha put this way:

*Do not dwell in the past. Do not dream of the future.*
*Concentrate the mind on the present moment.*

So I did concentrate, following Elizabeth's words as she said, "Ok, we begin the Floor Series with Wind Removing pose. Your heart rate should be back to normal, your breath silky smooth. Remember that the Standing Series is just a warm up. Now, as Bikram likes to say, the *real* yoga begins." Elizabeth's words echoed identically with those I had heard in Bozeman over and over again. I can't count the number of times I have cringed hearing that the Standing Series that just left me light-headed was "just a warm-up to the *real* yoga".

"Grab your right leg two inches beneath your knee," Elizabeth continued, "all ten fingers interlocked." Lying there on my back, finally relaxing and cooling after the rigors of the Standing Series, I realized that I love Wind

Removing pose because
it comes just at the
right time.  "Pull the
knee      toward      your
shoulder, avoiding your rib cage.  Left foot relaxed, left calf
on the ground, elbows pulled in close to your body, both
shoulders relaxed to the floor.  Pull your chin to your chest
and freeze.  You should be able to feel your hip joint
opening.  Freeze there...and release."

We repeated the pose with the left leg, then with both
legs pulled in to our chests.  Bikram says that the pose helps
the ascending colon (right leg), the descending colon (left
leg), and the transverse colon (both legs).  Help the colon
or not, the pose certainly comes by its name, Wind
Removing, honestly.  While it doesn't happen that often,
periodically in class the toot, toot, toot of a student
breaking wind can be heard.  Rarely does anyone laugh as
the name of the pose has made the actual event uneventful.
That is unless the passing gas comes out in exceptionally
thunderous proportions.

Then we all still giggle.

"Time for a sit up."  It was Elizabeth again, bringing us
out of *Savasana*, Dead Body pose, that Bikram mandates
between each set and pose in the Floor Series.  "Toes and
heels together" Elizabeth continued, "feet flexed, arms over
your head, cross your thumbs.  Now inhale, suck in your
stomach, and sit up!  Reach
forward and grab your toes,
elbows outside of your knees,
with a double exhale.  Try to

touch your forehead to your knees.  Good.  Now everyone turn around and lie down for *Bhujangasana*, Cobra pose."

Cobra pose starts a series of four poses collectively known as the Spine Strengthening Series, targeting the lower, middle, upper, and then entire spine.  Why such a focus?  Bikram provides a simple answer, noting that he is quoting his yogi when he says,

> *The spine is the source of all energy,*
> *the center of our human body's life...*
> *If you have a good spine, you'll have a good life.*

"Bring your legs and feet together," Elizabeth told us, "like a cobra tail.  Palms to the floor under your shoulders, all five fingers together.  Toes pointed; tighten your butt muscles; lock your knees.  Take a deep breath in, now look up at the ceiling and using the strength of your back lift your torso off the ground.  Remember this is a back up, not a push up.  We are strengthening the lumbar spine.  Elbows close to your sides, shoulders relaxed and down away from the ears.  Freeze here...and release.  Lower your head to  the mat, turn your face to the right and relax in *Savasana*— toes touching, heels falling apart, hands in close to the body, palms facing up."

*Savasana* here is on the belly and when I do it correctly I swear my body melts into the floor.  I love belly *Savasana*.  Twenty seconds later we did another set of Cobra, returned to *Savasana* looking to the left this time, and then moved on.

D epending on who you want to listen to, and what they choose to cite as evidence, yoga has been around for 4,000 to 8,000 years. Five thousand years seems to be the age that pops up most often, likely because a 5,000-year old carving from the Indus Valley (near the Pakistan-India border) shows what appears to be a yogi seated in a meditative posture.

Let's just say yoga is old.

Bikram runs with the 5,000 year claim. "What's right is what works," he says, "and yoga has been proven to work for 5,000 years." Bikram calls Patanjali[7] the "father of yoga", and the creator of the original of 84 *asanas* we recognize in Hatha yoga today. Likewise scholars credit Patanjali with being the author of the Yoga Sutras, the foundational text of yoga. The Sutras outline the principles and philosophy of yoga, plus give light to concepts like karma that permeate Indian thought.

Bikram claims that Patanjali and other ancient masters identified eight types of yoga. Not 20, as *Yoga Journal* suggests, just eight, and none of the eight is called Bikram's. Each of Bikram's eight yoga types has special characteristics and each focuses on separate aspects of the body, mind, and spirit:

1) *Karma*—yoga of action, work, and duty
2) *Hatha*—yoga of the physical practice
3) *Raja*—yoga of mental process and rational thought
4) *Vedanta*—yoga of philosophical grounding, including sharing of thoughts and ideas

---

[7] Patanjali lived in the second century BC.

5)  *Bhakti*—yoga of devotional practice
6)  *Mantra*—yoga of chanting and sound
7)  *Jnana*—yoga of attained knowledge
8)  *Laya*—yoga of the imagination and abstract thought

Of the eight forms of yoga, Bikram apparently sees his job as helping his students engage with the first three. He calls his classes 90-minute meditations "...combining Hatha and Raja Yoga—and you can bet you're performing some concentrated Karma Yoga as well." To truly practice Karma Yoga, per Bikram, one must prepare the body through Hatha Yoga and the mind through Raja Yoga.

Hatha Yoga operates on the physical plane, in other words it is what most of us think of when we hear the word "yoga". Hatha provides for physical strengthening and purification as a method of preparing the body and mind for meditation. The word Hatha derives from the Sanskrit *Ha*, meaning sun, and *Tha*, meaning moon. The sun and the moon are symbolic of the balance practitioners seek through Hatha Yoga, the balance of strength and flexibility, the balance of body, mind, and spirit.

Bikram has particularly harsh words for those changes wrought on Hatha Yoga when it arrived in the USA from India, including for those Indian yogis who brought it across the Pacific:

> How did they screw up their sacred duty? First, they changed
> some of Patanjali's original 84 postures to accommodate the
> inflexibility of American bodies, and stopped teaching other
> postures they thought would be too hard...Americans, they
> mistakenly believed, should not be pushed out of their
> "comfort zone". Next came all the bizarre props, including

*ropes, straps, chairs, pulleys….All of this compromised the true way and diluted Hatha Yoga.*

Bikram extends his harsh words equally to the new teachers in America:

*The dilution that these yogis caused was passed down to their disciples…who became teachers themselves. These American teachers then proceeded to take yoga even further in the wrong direction… American yoga teachers invented posture after posture, modification after modification, making up their own Sanskrit names, and then selling their defective wares to the uninitiated…These days, the yoga "brands" are getting even more ridiculous; you've got Easy Yoga, Sit-at-Your-Desk Yoga, Yoga for Beginners, Yoga for Dummies, Yoga for Pets, and Babaar Yoga. It's all Mickey Mouse Yoga to me….there is only Hatha. Bikram Yoga is Hatha Yoga.*

Raja Yoga, as defined in the Yoga Sutras, operates on the mental plane. Think of Hatha yoga as being of the body, Raja Yoga as being of the mind. In theory we cannot arrive at a place of controlling the conscious mind (i.e., Raja Yoga) without the physical calm and subsequent mental discipline achieved through Hatha Yoga. Here's how the Bhagavad Gita, one of the most sacred scriptures of Hinduism, puts it:

*When, through the practice of yoga,
the mind ceases its restless movements, and becomes still,
the aspirant realizes the [Soul].*

You remember the whole chirping cricket thing, right?

Karma Yoga speaks to your life path, achieving that for which you were put on the Earth, achieving your destiny.

Karma alone is generally thought of as the sum of all your work, deeds, actions, and experiences. Sogyal Rinpoche says that in the West we often misunderstand karma to mean fate or predestination. Instead, he says, it should be looked at as an infallible law of cause and effect:

*The word karma literally means "action," and karma is both the power latent within actions, and the results our actions bring…It means that whatever we do, with our body, speech, or mind, will have a corresponding result. Each action, even the smallest, is pregnant with its consequences… [As Buddha] said: "Do not overlook tiny good actions, thinking they are of no benefit; even tiny drops of water in the end will fill a huge vessel."*

Karma Yoga has been described as the path of dedicated work. The key here is that the work is not self-serving, but instead provided as a selfless offering to others, to your God, or to the Self within (as opposed to the self—small "s"—or equivalently the ego; think here again of the Self equaling the Soul or the Spirit). Mata Amritanandamayi, a contemporary Hindu spiritual leader, ties it all together by saying,

*Our compassion and acts of selflessness take us to the deeper truths. Through selfless action we can eradicate the ego that conceals the Self. Detached, selfless action leads to liberation. Such action is not just work; it is karma yoga.*

After a couple of days break in Corvallis, we climbed in to the car to drive to Portland and Oregon Health & Science University for Kate's surgery the following day. We planned to spend the night in a hotel,

like we do when Kate has an appointment at OHSU, then
take an aerial tram—that's right, just like at a ski area—up
to the hospital.

The tram thing is weird, I know, but understand that
Portland Oregon has the best public transportation of any
American city I have ever visited, including a spectacular
aerial tram that connects the South Waterfront District
along the Willamette River to Marquam Hill, where the
main OHSU hospital and campus are located. Tram cars
soar directly across Interstate 5, supported by a massive
silver tower sitting right next to the highway. Think of the
biggest aerial tramway you've ever seen, perhaps at the ski
area of Jackson Hole or Chamonix. Now to get the full
picture remove the snow and add rain...*lots* of rain.

As Kate and I were driving up I-5 and into Portland,
the tram came into view directly ahead, high overhead. Six
weeks earlier, as part of our travel between doctors'
appointments, we had taken the tram up from the
Waterfront District to OHSU. It had been a windy day
with the tram car almost empty. Suddenly a gust hit us
from the side swinging our tram car enough to bring a
nervous "Whoa!" from the few on board.

"Not to worry," the tram operator had said. "The
wind would have to come up a fair piece from here before
we'd even need to slow down, much less close the tram.
You'll be alright."

On this day, far below in our car, Kate and I crossed
under the tram, talking little, instead just holding hands and
worrying.

The wind, for the moment, held calm.

# Chapter 8

# An Empty Canvas

*Life is a great canvas;*
*throw on all the paint you can.*

—Danny Kaye

I once went to one of those expensive corporate seminars where a motivational speaker charged $400 per person per day to teach 20 of us how to better reach our potential. After 16 hours of training the only one reaching their potential, as far as I could see, was the speaker, who would clear over $15,000 for the two day course. It's not hard to see why the speaker was so motivated.

Fifteen years later I *do* recall one thing from that course, however, so *maybe* it was worth it. I remember the visualization the speaker provided about how good things come effortlessly to us when we commit to a goal. He said, "Once you declare yourself a runway, people will try to land on you. For example, if you say, 'I am going to travel to Honduras and build homes with Habitat for Humanity', suddenly people will arrive from out of the

woodwork to tell you about their own experience with
Habitat for Humanity, their travels to Honduras and an
ancient ruin that you must visit while you are there, or the
address of their nephew living in Utila who would be a
great contact for you.    The world and its resources
suddenly open up to you just because of your declaration of
intent."

While the speaker's meaning was clear, I found his
airplanes-landing-on-a-runway metaphor a bit forced.    I
remember thinking that he would have been better off to
have selected a canvas, saying something more like, "Once
you declare yourself committed to an idea you become an
empty canvas that people will come to paint on."    Same
idea, just a bit more eloquent.    I wonder if anyone would
pay me $15,000 for that pearl of wisdom.

Paralleling my thoughts, the philosopher Osho once
said,

> *Life in itself is an empty canvas,*
> *it becomes whatsoever you paint on it.*
> *You can paint misery, you can paint bliss.*
> *The freedom is your glory.*

Osho's message tells us that responsibility for our state of
being, our state of happiness, rests with us alone.

Another reason I like the canvas metaphor is that
unlike a runway a canvas can be readily replaced, allowing
you to start anew over and over and over again.    It's
important to realize that starting anew does not devalue
that which you've created before.    Indeed those paintings
can be set aside to cherish and remember.    Likewise there

may be paintings that we simply abandon, sometimes even in an incomplete form.

Starting with a fresh canvas reopens the world to its infinite possibilities.

We arrived at the hospital at 6 AM for Kate's surgery. By 6:30 Dr. Daneshmand arrived at pre-op with the news that Kate's blood levels had taken a terrible turn overnight, indicating a real concern for her kidney health. I did not like the strained look on his face.

The surgery took almost five hours. Depending on the surgical outcome, our life would start anew or be pushed toward despair. I paced the halls through the entire thing, I tried my best to breathe, and I prayed.

Kate's oncologist, who was not part of the surgical team, nonetheless went in and out of the surgery throughout the morning and periodically came to the waiting area to tell Kate's parents, Giff and Ellen, plus Suz, Dennis, and me that all was proceeding well. Sometime past noon Dr. Daneshmand came out from the operating theater, smiling, happy, and he hugged me. An honest, sincere and, I think, relieved hug.

It went perfectly, he said.

In the days after Kate's surgery I was back at a Bikram's studio, this time at John's Landing along the Willamette River. I had picked the studio[8] a month earlier due to its proximity—just a tram ride and a mile

---

[8] Portland has four Bikram's studios.

walk—to OHSU.    Kate's parents would sit with her, so
each day for the week she stayed in the hospital I packed up
my gear and headed down the hill to continue my
Challenge.

Like Elizabeth, Christy, the John's Landing studio
owner, kindly offered me a student rate due to my odd
Challenge travel schedule between Bozeman, Corvallis, and
Portland.[9]    Within a couple of days there in Portland I
crossed Day 30, the half way point of my Challenge.  Now,
instead of counting up to 60 each day, I happily found
myself counting backwards from 30 but, truth be told, the
end still looked a mighty long ways away.

As in Corvallis, I felt immediately comfortable at
Christy's studio—knowing the poses already, feeling the
camaraderie of shared experience with my fellow students,
being included in a couple of fun celebrations Christy put
on for her students.    And on Week 6/Day 33 of my
Challenge I also felt something else: wet and uncomfortable
before we even started.  And not wet from sweating early
on.    Instead, in western Oregon's humidity neither my
towel underfoot nor the clammy shorts I pulled on had
dried since the previous day's class.

As if sensing my discomfort, Louis, one of Christy's
teachers, said, "We should never be upset by our
limitations.  They are, after all, what brought us to this
place."

They tell you to listen and listen hard in yoga class.  It

---

[9] One of the benefits of doing the Challenge through just one studio is
that the studio generally offers a greatly reduced fee per class.

helps you focus on the mechanical tasks at hand. But you can learn simple yet profound truths while you are listening, as well, and I would find Louis's classes regularly sprinkled with such wisdom.

Louis worked us through Cobra, *Savasana*, and then a sit up. "Now turn around and lie down for *Salabhasana*, Locust pose."

The pose starts with you on your belly, simple enough, but then comes an onerous command. "Place your arms under your body," Louis said. "Your arms should be open and down like you're bumping a volleyball. Palms flat on the floor; elbows close together; pinky fingers touching. Your arms should be pinned under your body, your feet touching together." I twisted myself into this ridiculous shape, elbows, wrists, and shoulders screaming out in pain.

Holding this awkward position, Bikram has you raise first your right leg, knee locked (what else?!), and hold for ten seconds, then repeat with the left leg. Finally comes the coup de grâce. Louis continued, "Place your mouth to the towel. Don't move it. This is to protect your neck. Readjust your arms—see if you can get your elbows all the way in to touch each other. Lock your knees and point your toes. Your hips, butt, and thigh muscles should be engaged. Now without lifting your head, take a big inhale, squeeze your legs together, and lift both legs off the floor as high as possible."

The double leg lift is tough, so tough that Bikram calls it the part of

his entire class students hate most. Louis again: "Remember what Bikram says, 'The right way is the hard way.'"

I rolled that idea around in my mind a while not quite sure what Louis or Bikram meant. I just knew that right there, right then, two legs up in the air, elbows aflame, I took solace in the fact that I *must* have been doing it the right way because whatever I was doing was *really* hard.

In a moment, however, Louis destroyed my fantasy, saying, "Scott, lock your knees. If form is lost, you lose all benefit. Better to just lift both legs an inch off the ground if that's all you can do."

Coming out of the second round of Locust into *Savasana* several folks around the room grunted in exasperation, including me. As blood rushed back into our aching wrists , Louis asked us to try to come out of the pose in the same way we went in, with ease and grace.

Then he added quietly, "Remember, it's not about strength but instead it's about what we are willing to endure."

After we rested for 20 seconds in belly *Savasana* Louis said, "Next *Poorna-Salabhasana*, Full Locust pose. We now work on the middle spine. Arms straight out, palms facing down, chin on the floor. Legs together and tightened, point your toes, now take a big inhale and lift everything—arms, legs, head, feet—off the ground. Lift up, come up, fly up! Arms up and back like you are a 747. Fingertips level with the head. Fly! That's beautiful. Now freeze...hold it...and release to

*Savasana*, head turned to the right."

For a time when I started my yoga practice, I used to think that at this point we were doing "Lotus" and "Full Lotus" poses (sorry, I wasn't smart enough to know that Lotus is the classic cross-legged sitting pose we so often associate with a wizened yogi meditating on a mountaintop). So whether I heard I was flying like a 747 or not, I kept visualizing myself as a beautiful, blossoming flower. Then one day an instructor said, "Locust, you know like a grasshopper." I almost deflated in mid-pose. Suddenly the soft petals of the flower turned to scaly hind legs and segmented abdomen of an insect, and an ugly one at that. Suddenly my vision of the peace and bouquet and beauty of the pose turned to thoughts of swarms and plagues and pestilence.

No matter what they tell you, sometimes it's better not to listen.

S omebody I think a lot of people wished they hadn't listened to was Osho. It was Osho who earlier told us that we have a choice about coloring our life's canvas with misery or bliss. That is such a fine visualization. So why do I say that folks wished they hadn't listened to him? Because Osho (don't you always feel a little uncomfortable with folks who claim to have only a single name?) is a guy who was also once known as Bhagwan Shree Rajneesh.

Remember the Bhagwan? The guy who in 1981 established the City of Rajneeshpuram in the rural Oregon, who collected Rolls Royces like they were bottle caps, who because of his controversial views on sex became known as the "sex guru", and who perhaps not coincidentally gathered legions of followers that threw their life savings and—I'm thinking aloud here—intellectual capabilities to the wind.

In just four short years, a time during which angry Oregonians were looking for any excuse to run the thousands of Rajneeshies out of the state, Rajneeshpuram imploded. And the Rajneeshies—possibly acting separately from the Bhagwan—did it to themselves, committing several serious crimes including perpetrating a salmonella attack on the citizens of The Dalles.

In case you follow this sort of stuff, Bhagwan Shree Rajneesh is the very same guy who was born Chandra Mohan Jain, then did a stint as Acharya Rajneesh before giving Bhagwan a try. I'm not sure about the other name changes, but the switch to Osho followed the whole poisoning-a-community thing and thus seems somewhat understandable.

Less glibly, for bioterrorism is surely no joke, the Bhagwan obviously had a way of reinventing himself into a new persona when he felt the need. He did not always go for a complete makeover, however. Whatever his name, Bhagwan...er...Osho continued to amass devotees as an Indian philosopher and mystic well known for his thoughtful and often challenging insights. So well known, in fact, that Osho is one of only two authors whose entire works have been placed in New Delhi at the Library of India's National Parliament. And he's keeping pretty good company; the other author is Mahatma Gandhi.

Osho's book titles include <u>My Way, the Way of the White Clouds</u>, <u>From Sex to Superconsciousness</u>, and <u>Joy: The Happiness That Comes From Within</u>. In the latter book Osho proves that he clearly had a thing for the canvas and paint as a metaphor for life. Here he tells us that if we are seeking happiness and it proves elusive then we should

> ...do something that has nothing to do with happiness. Paint. You need not learn painting; can't you throw color on a canvas? Any child can do it. Just throw color on a canvas and you may be surprised: You are not a painter, but something beautiful happens.

I like that idea, don't you? How many times have you happily surprised yourself after trying something you had no idea of how to undertake at the outset? The canvas may be empty today but it doesn't have to be tomorrow.

Simply starting is the key.

Perhaps 100 miles east of the OSHU hospital as a crow might fly—and that crow would have to fly mighty high to get over Mount Hood—sits the former site of Rajneeshpuram. Kate and I had driven through the town site once in the early 90s and seen little other than abandoned buildings and a lone antelope. We had been headed into Eastern Oregon, bound for a long hike in the mountains.

Our long hikes for the moment led from Kate's hospital bed down the hall at OHSU, up an elevator, then across a lengthy sky bridge that hangs high above the city lights of Portland. Day by day as she healed the walks got longer and stronger. Often we'd be gone an hour.

Sometimes on our walks we sat in the hallways along the way to rest and watch the workings of the hospital. Administrators, families, doctors, nurses, students, and EMTs variously sauntered or dashed to their next appointments. Kate and I looked on in sadness each time a young child suffering from cancer came by in a wheelchair or on a gurney. Possibly some of them might never have a chance to complete their life's first painting, much less have the opportunity to pull out a blank canvas and start anew.

"It's not about strength," Louis had said, "but instead it's about what we are willing to endure." But what if we're *not* willing? What if we never asked to play in the game?

One morning Kate's surgeon, Sia Daneshmand, came in after a weekend away, a weekend in which his residents looked after her. Sia was almost bursting with joy, having just seen Kate's most recent blood results. The number that had caused him such concern just before surgery had rebounded dramatically, almost back into the normal range, to a new place where Kate had not been for a very long time.

This is a good man, a man not afraid to share his emotions. I don't recall if the three of us high-fived, but even if we didn't the feeling in that moment was the same.

"I have an idea," Sia said, eyes sparkling. "I think we're going to take you off the kidney transplant list and put you on the kidney donor list instead!"

# Chapter 9

# Firm Fixation

*Every obstacle yields to stern resolve.*
*He who is fixed to a star does not change his mind.*

—Leonardo da Vinci

S itting side by side in the passenger seat of my car, the rolled up yoga mat and the hunting rifle made for odd company. I had just finished an evening yoga class, then pointed myself toward a distant set of mountains in Central Montana. The mat had started in my gym bag but part way down the highway I thought better of it and unpacked my shorts and towel onto the seat back so that they might dry. In the process of emptying the bag, I dropped the mat alongside the thirty-ought-six, grabbed my half-full water bottle, took a swig, then set it on the seat as well, being careful not to bang the rifle scope.

It had been years, probably 25, since I last shot a deer, although my Dad, brother, and I used to hunt all through my youth. Hunting season in those days usually ended with a much anticipated family feast at Wong's in Billings, where they would cook our wild game into delectable dishes like sweet and sour pheasant, Moo Goo grouse, Kung Pao duck, and Mu Shu venison.

After I left my folks' home in Billings, I also soon left Montana. During the intervening 20 years I stopped hunting, partially because I didn't feel comfortable doing so in the more crowded states I moved to, partially because I became interested in trying other things out like doing yoga, being a vegetarian, fly fishing fanatically, backpacking and bicycle touring and sea kayaking in strange places, and stringing words together into uncomfortably long sentences for others to read. Oh yea, and I met Kate, who runs for the back forty at the sight of a gun.

However being back in Montana, as we had been for ten years, had a way of evoking my hunting heritage. Sure hunting here is omnipresent—how many convenience stores near where you live sell hunting rifles? We got one here. But what gave me the urge to return to hunting was not just a gun-loving convenience store owner. No, instead what can really drive a man to hunt again is all those dinner gatherings where your manly friends show up with slabs of bloody elk and you...well...you arrive with a pallid cube of tofu. Over the years I've heard a lot of folks ooh and aah over bloody elk, but not once over soybean curd. I know, I know, I can hear you now—I already tried bringing marinated tempeh instead. Impressive, yes, but somehow not quite the same cachet as "last year's elk".

So I decided to hunt again.

For two years I had simply gone out and walked around the woods, seeing deer but never feeling like I had a shot that assured a clean kill. That was, and always had been, my goal: one shot, clean kill, dead animal.

My first hunting trip, one of those unsuccessful ones, back in the fold did not go smoothly. Kate and our friend DeeAnn needed the small four-wheel drive car Kate and I share, so I had to borrow DeeAnn's vehicle, an equally small rear-wheel drive pickup. Let me tell you something about DeeAnn. While she is a dirt-of-the-Earth South Dakota farm girl, I think it's fair to say that no one expects her to be back on a tractor soon. Instead, along with being a passionate defender of abused kids as her profession and an avid outdoorswoman in her free time, DeeAnn is a feminist to be reckoned with.

Thus it was that on my way back from my first hunt in over 20 years I parked DeeAnn's toy pickup in the empty parking lot of a small town gas station. The pickup's side panels were covered in mud from earlier in the day. The rear window of DeeAnn's pickup topper was also covered, though with bumper stickers that formed a billboard to her life:

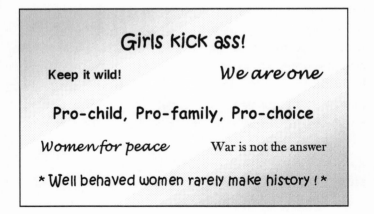

Girls kick ass!

Keep it wild!                    We are one

Pro-child, Pro-family, Pro-choice

Women for peace        War is not the answer

* Well behaved women rarely make history ! *

While I hadn't even had the excitement of *seeing* a deer
in three or four hikes that day, I did come very close to
sliding off a greasy, muddy, rain-slickened back road.
Fishtailing about I had sent up a silent prayer: Please God
keep me out of the ditch. Please don't let me have to ask
some gruff old Montana rancher to tie up his tow rope to
the hitch right under DeeAnn's personal sandwich board.

Thankfully, although I covered the little pickup in
mud, I managed to avoid a run in with a rancher in a big
Ford F350. But at the gas station just such a monster
pickup pulled in next to DeeAnn's toy truck soon after I
stepped into the shop for coffee. The tire on this behemoth
stood as tall as DeeAnn's hood. Two orange coated
hunters descended from the monster truck—they didn't
use a rope ladder to climb down, but they could have.

The next time I looked up the two had paused behind
DeeAnn's pickup, reading her life's philosophies. A surly
glance passed between the men before they made their way
to come inside. But then their crusty looks turned slightly
befuddled as they passed the passenger door, seeing my
rifle sitting on the car seat.

Inside, I pulled my hat lower over my eyes but as I was
the only customer in the convenience store, and wearing
hunters' orange to boot, I had no place to run to, no place
to hide. I decided the best defense would be a strong
offense so I grabbed my coffee and met them at the entry.
Holding the door open for them to pass I asked cheerfully,
"So, you get your deer yet?"

Now, two years later, I had my own vehicle—not a
bumper sticker in sight—and I had a plan. After hitting

yoga hard, I planned to drive late to a trailhead on public
land, sleep in the car, rise before sunrise, grab the rifle,
hike into the bush in search of a young mule deer buck,
shoot it with a single well-placed shot, clean the deer, and
be home by two.

And that's exactly what I did.

At sunrise I walked quietly along, hidden by trees,
until just over a rise I saw my deer lying down on an open
hillside 100 yards away.  I snuck on my hands and knees
just out of the trees to where I could line up the shot,
stabilizing the rifle on my pack.  I stared through the scope
with steely resolve.  Not "steely" in the strong or manly
sense, but instead steely because I was fixated on the idea
that this would be a clean, exact, quick-killing shot or I
simply would not take it.  I aimed.  I readjusted my
position.  I aimed again, sweat now on my brow.

And then I shot.  The deer stood up, and fell dead.

So my plan was great and it worked perfectly but
here's what I had conveniently forgotten over the years of
not hunting:  cleaning a big dead animal is a messy affair.
First you have to lay the dead deer on its back—nose,
chest, and abdomen facing skyward.  Then you must kneel
down next to the animal and cut through fur and then skin.
Once through the skin surprisingly little happens, no blood,
no guts, no real gore.  Instead you next have to begin
slicing away the fascia, the endless bands and sheets of
tissue that connect the skin to the muscles of the body
cavity.

Skin sufficiently separated away, you make a cut
through the abdominal muscles that opens the entire body

cavity. In an instant the stench of hot blood and entrails overwhelms you, reminding you that this is no longer the beautiful, living being it had been 20 minutes before, but is instead now a large dead body staring off into nothingness. The cutting continues, through more tissue connecting the organs to each other and to the protective rib cage. Blood becomes prevalent. And then at some point, the whole messy affair piles out onto the ground.

When this explosion of entrails occurred with my deer, I jumped back barely able to make it out of the way because of wobbly knees aching from 15 minutes of kneeling. For a moment I felt overwhelmed: the awful smell, those lifeless brown eyes, the gut pile on the ground...and then the realization that I had to drag this big animal two miles back to the car.

My first deer in 25 years. I found a nearby rock and sat down to consider the awful barbarity, and yet somehow at the same time the peaceful sanctity, of the moment.

I needed to breathe.

I filled my lungs, holding my breath for a long time before exhaling slowly. I closed my eyes and gave silent thanks to the deer at my feet—for the food it would provide me, for the connection to the Earth it gave me.

K ate's determination to return to her life helped us quickly exit the hospital. We stayed in Portland for a few days, taking tentative steps into the real world, including life-affirming visits with friends from Portland, friends traveling through, and Kate's folks.

Mostly Kate slept or held tight to her place in bed,

sending me off to do yoga at Christy's or pick up some exotic food item that inevitably went uneaten. A box arrived from a half-dozen Bozeman friends filled with good wishes and gifts. Kate read the cards and thumbed through several intriguing books. We took photos of each wearing a set of silly Dracula teeth Chris and Rebekah had sent along. We tried to look scary but that's tough to do while laughing aloud.

In a few more days we moved back to Corvallis, our idea being to stay there for another three weeks to be sure Kate felt sufficiently recovered before we returned home to Montana. Friends Randy and Kelly loaned us their house while they traveled in an act of great humanity. In those weeks so many kindnesses from friends and family again anchored Kate as she continued to gain strength.

Shared laughter, walks, time, love—they all matter.

G iven our return to Corvallis I quickly found myself back at Elizabeth's studio. Week 7/Day 41 of my Challenge, Thanksgiving Day. What better time to give thanks than with Kate healing and getting stronger by the day? And what better way could there be to start Thanksgiving Day than with a 9 AM yoga class? None, apparently, as the class is packed wall to wall.

Erika teaches on this day. Although I have not met her, I am already enamored with Erika from my first stops into the Corvallis studio before Kate's surgery. Back then someone told me that Erika had done yoga each and every day for over two years! When I met her on this day I had to ask, "Or so *you're* Erika. Aren't you the one who's done seven hundred days of yoga in a row?"

"Actually, seven hundred fifty-five," she says matter of factly.

Gulp.

All I can think to say in reply is, "Hey, but who's counting, right?"

Wow 60 days of yoga in 70 suddenly seems so puny. I slink into the studio, plop down my mat, lay back, and stare at the ceiling hoping to find the figure of a Cheshire Cat I can fixate on.

By the time we make it through the Standing Series and into the Floor Series I can pretty much guess how Erika managed to practice yoga non-stop for over 700 days: discipline. She is the single most militaristic, order-barking instructor I've had. If Marine drill sergeants ever get a hankering to try a yoga class, I'm guessing they would feel right at home with Erika pacing the studio in front of them. But they better come ready because I'm also guessing that she would kick their collective asses.

I love Erika's class.

"All right," she is saying just now, "final pose in the Spine Strengthening Series, *Dhanurasana*. We've strengthened the lower, middle, and upper spine. Now we tie them all together with Bow Pulling pose. Chin forward. Everyone reach back and grab your feet two inches below the toes, NO higher, NO lower. Feet six inches apart. All five fingers together. I want to see everyone with the thumb included with the grip. EVERYONE!"

When I first started Bikram Yoga I always hated even just this set up to the pose. For a time I worried that because of my bad left knee I would not be able to grab both feet simultaneously. Indeed in those days my surgery knee would not bend much so I took to reaching back and grabbing my left calf before inching my way down to the proper foothold. Ugly but effective.

But that was then. Now I grab both ankles with only a single mini-grunt.

"Now inhale deeply," Erika continues, walking through the class while periodically consulting her wristwatch, "and lift up, GO UP, point your toes, look up to the ceiling. Come up, higher, Higher, HIGHER! Roll forward onto the soft of your belly. NO bent wrists. Don't pull with your arms but instead kick up with your legs. KICK UP! Someday you'll be able to see your feet rise right up above your head. Now look up, one notch higher…higher    still…hold    it…Hold It…HOLD IT!"

Erika's voice rises to a crescendo as the pose nears its climax, then she ends with a quieter, "…and release into *Savasana*."

We complete a second set of Bow pose and then arrive at my arch nemesis: Fixed Firm pose, aka *Supta-Vajrasana*. Sadly, it's that knee thing again. You know, the one I mentioned I worry about continuously, the one from a skiing accident over 30 years ago that still shows the marks of 20 stitches along a ten-inch scar. Here is a pose that is totally passive, that has you do nothing more than simply sit

back on your knees. It's a pose that a
pre-schooler can do. In fact most kids
can lay all the way down onto their
backs no problem.    Heck, most of
them could play a Nintendo game for an hour there. Easy
for them, yes, but I've seen the pose make grown men
cry—trust me on this.

The term "Fixed Firm" isn't particularly clear to me.
*Fixed* to the floor?  Maybe.  *Firm* in my conviction that
attempting this pose is the stupidest idea I've ever had?
Perhaps.  A glossary of words used in the Gnostic Dharma
says that *Vajrasana* is a pose in which the practitioner is
steady and firm, where the knees become "hard" and the
spine becomes "firm and strong"[10].  Still not that clear, at
least not to me.  So let's look at the Sanskrit translations for
help.  Apparently *Supta* means reclining, *Vajr* means man or
hero and comes from the same Latin root as virile, and
*asana* means pose.

Now *that* helps; I'm all in favor of being a virile hero
lying on the floor in fetching repose.

Virile or not, my injured knee is throbbing.  In fact it
has been throbbing in preparation of this moment ever
since we dropped to the floor a half dozen poses ago.
That's right, while it's counter to all that quiet-the-
chirping-cricket advice, I often count my way towards

---

[10] The same glossary defines Gnostic Dharma as "the acquisition of
personal experience, but in relation with our own psychology, in relation
with how the planet functions, how life is, the truth of all the mysteries of
life and death, and the practical facts of how life and death move and
flow." I just thought you might want to know.

Fixed Firm, knowing that if I survive the pose, I will survive the class.

Oddly, the anticipation is not driven simply by dread, but also by some sort of a peculiar fascination with the great unknown potential of my body. Will I touch my back to the floor today? Will today be the first day ever that my knees don't cry out in pain? Or instead will I get stuck in the pose and need a winch to be lifted out? It's the same feeling of dread mixed with fascination that writer Collin Fletcher once spoke of this way:

*And it is the unknown, above all,*
*that scares the living daylights out of us—*
*and draws us like moths to its candle.*

After having us come out of *Savasana* and do a sit up, the time comes. Erika says, "Come to the top of your mat and towel for Fixed Firm pose, *Supta-Vajrasana*. Kneeling position, feet flat to the floor, soles of the feet facing up. Everyone start with your knees together, feet together, then spread your feet to hip-width apart. Sit down until your butt touches the floor between your feet."

I'm feeling discomfort already even though the posture has barely started. And not just in the knees but my ankles call out as well, rebelling against their flattened state, against their blood supply being cut off, against their connective tissues being torn apart.

Oblivious to my plight, Erika marches on: "Reach back and place your hands on your feet, fingers facing forward. Slowly bend your right elbow and then left elbow to the floor. Let your head hang back. *Go only as far as your body will allow you today.* Remember this is our only passive posture in class. And remember what Bikram says, 'You can mess with the gods, but you can't mess with the knees.'"

I lower myself down just as described, though Erika's words say nothing of the ripping fascia in my left knee and both hips. I feel myself being torn apart, but it is not the feeling of a muscle or tendon tear. Instead I feel my ankles, knees, and hips being pulled and rearranged and renewed in a way that surely causes pain, though not searing, single point pain such as comes with something like an abrupt hamstring pull in a track meet.

I pause at this point to reflect on Chris's oft-repeated, cautionary words during Fixed Firm: "As in life, here sometimes less is more."

Before I can decide if I am ready to proceed or should just hang out here for the day, Erika continues, "Now, if you can, drop your head to the mat, then your shoulders and torso, lowering everything to the floor. Slide your elbows out from under you and raise your arms up over your head, grabbing opposite elbows. Tuck your chin to your chest and hold it." She looks at her watch and begins the 20 second count recommended by Bikram.

I decide to go, as the years of Bikram Yoga and the days of the Challenge have been good to me in this pose. I am grateful as we proceed because at each step of the pose I am able to follow and at least marginally complete Erika's instructions.

I am lying on my back now, butt and shoulders touching the ground, arms overhead, and every single time

I successfully arrive here I marvel at the body that I have begun to reclaim.  On my first day in Bikram Yoga I could barely sit back to 90 degrees, much less put my butt to the ground, much less drop my back to the floor.  In the 30-plus years since my skiing accident I had long ago given up on ever sitting back on my knees again.  But by a year after I started Bikram's I had made it to my elbows, head dangling back.  A year later, on the first day I touched my shoulders to the ground and lay on my back, I cried.  Real tears.  No sound.  No one knew.

It was a singular moment of intense, honest joy.

**"N**o pain, no gain."  Bikram claims that saying is one of the most important lessons he has learned in America.  Pain like I feel in Fixed Firm pose, he explains, is simply a part of yoga.  Understand pain, work with pain, use pain to improve your body, Bikram says, because pain can be your ally:

> *Of course it hurts!  Contrary to popular belief, pain often means that you are doing something right.  Be grateful and be patient.  Nobody's telling you to be a martyr or a masochist; I'm just talking about going one small step beyond discomfort.  Stretch to the point at which you feel pain, the threshold, and learn from it.*

It's clear that pain in yoga is most often associated with the stretching of long contracted muscles and tendons, and to the tearing down of the webbing of inter-tied fascia that holds this physical being we call our body together:  our skin to our muscles, our muscles to our bones, our organs to each other.

"Tissue is the issue," said one instructor.

Pathologists use the word "fixation" to describe their efforts to preserve tissue. Their goal is to keep tissue from decaying, to keep it as close as possible to its natural state. That seems a morbid but apt analogy for the tissue work going on in Fixed Firm and other poses.

But maybe this is a better analogy. When I lay back in Fixed Firm I feel like the inner tube in a bicycle tire must feel. (Granted one might ask, "Does an inner tube actually have feelings?") When you pump up an inner tube the pressure builds and builds until soon it is pushed against the container of the tire wall, stretching, straining to expand, but held in by the tire. The pressure builds and builds but the tube will not explode because you can withdraw the air pump at any moment.

In the same way in yoga you can push harder and harder and feel the pain and pressure grow. In Fixed Firm, for example, the further back you drop the more tension and stress and pull you feel in your ankles, knees, hips, and back. You can feel your body changing: muscles, ligaments, tendons, and fascia tearing away from each other, pressing against the container that is your skin. But as with filling the inner tube yoga builds stress, pressure, and change in your body *slowly*; there is little danger of injury because you are in control of when to stop.

As another instructor once said, "Anatomy is destiny." Agreed. But yoga provides us a way to change our body's destiny. At least a bit.

L et's say you've been practicing with Mr. Choudhury for several years and felt your own destiny changing: positive changes in your body, possibly in your mind as well, maybe even in your spirit. You've started coming to the studio multiple times a week, feel bad when you miss class, maybe have even once completed the 60-day Challenge. Maybe twice. You've begun to accept the oft-stated idea that "Yoga *is* life". What you've done has so inspired you that you want to continue on, to move even further into the fold.

If so, you may chose to deepen your practice, perhaps coming to class daily, studying the Yoga Sutras, building your life around yoga. Or you may choose, as many do, to become a certified Bikram's teacher. But if that's your path get ready—Bikram's teacher training is a massive undertaking on multiple levels.

Let's start with the financial. This year's class costs $6,600. A room at the hotel the training is taking place at will set you back $3,900 for the length of the course. But that's for a double. If you don't want to smell someone else's sweaty gym trunks drying every night better bump that up; you'll need to set aside $8,000 for a private room. Oh yea, and drop any thoughts of camping as housing at the hotel is mandatory. Food, at least per the official Bikram Yoga website, appears not to be included. We'll probably be eating lightly so let's add just $600. Likewise travel to Acapulco, site of this spring's training, is not included. Just for grins let's add $800 to get there (hey, I don't know where you are coming from). That totals to as much as $16,000 to become a certified instructor.

It's a lot, I know, but give me a break, it *is* Acapulco after all.

The sixteen grand doesn't include lost wages—assuming you already work—for the two months required to complete the training. That's right, eight weeks away from home, from early April to early June.

Feeling a little intimidated yet? Heck, that's just the financial underpinnings. The real challenge must surely be the training itself: 9 AM to 10:30 PM (and often much later by all reports), five days a week for eight weeks straight. Saturdays include a single 90-minute yoga class. Sundays Bikram lets you recover.

Bikram has said, "...practice requires discipline." And he clearly practices what he preaches. According to the teacher training course syllabus, aspiring teachers put in 13 or 14 hour days that include two daily Bikram classes (mandatory), posture clinics (mandatory), and anatomy lectures (mandatory). The only schedule items that appear to be optional are eating, sleeping, and showering.

Somewhere in there they obviously fit in some rigorous Dialogue training, as well. After laboring under some 40 or 50 instructors over four years I've found the Dialogue to be perhaps 98% consistent teacher-to-teacher, studio-to-studio. That's impressive for anybody's army.

Absorbing the Dialogue and graduating as a Bikram instructor results in a number of perks. With Bikram studios around the world, opportunities to travel and teach abound. Websites list full or temporary job openings, not to mention clinics in exotic places. Thus your teacher today may say that tomorrow s/he is flying off for a gig in

Australia or Costa Rica or Ireland, Berlin or Capetown or Kuala Lumpur.

Last year's teacher training took place in Hawaii. I found it both fun and strangely comforting to know that two trainees from Corvallis, Alex and Kacie, were in the midst of eight weeks of torture with two trainees, Jessie and Even, I knew of from Bozeman. That is the power of a vibrant yoga community.

While I would take classes from both newly certified Corvallis teachers before we left Oregon, I got an early peek into Alex's psyche from an email he sent to Elizabeth and that she shared in class. It had been the season of All Saints Day and Elizabeth had already sparked the crowd by bringing us out of *Savasana* to find that she had quietly slipped into a mischievous smile *and* a set of blood-red devil's horns. She was carrying a rubber trident that she prodded us with during the next pose. When we rested in *Savasana* again, many of us chuckling, Elizabeth said that she had just received an email from Alex at teacher training and that given the season she wanted to share it with us.

"Most of you know Alex," Elizabeth said, "but in case you don't all you need to know is that he is tall, slim, has short hair, and is extremely fit." And then she read:

*Wednesday was Halloween, I decided to dress up in wonderful style. Imagine, if you dare, a curly blond wig, a floral two piece Shakti yoga outfit with socks that gave me a perky B cup [to go with my] sweaty hairy legs. I set my mind to leave the wig on and socks in for the entire class, and in my determined and stubborn fashion I succeeded and actually had a really strong class, must have had something*

*to do with being in the second row and looking like a*
*muscular girl....*

*I must say I gained a new appreciation for women, so many*
*of the postures posing new challenges when there are boobs*
*in front, although it was a little easier to lift*
*my chest up in Full Locust because I had a*
*little elevation already from my implants.*

So sure yoga *is* life. I'm willing to buy into that sentiment, even if I'm not quite sure exactly what it means. Perhaps it means discipline? Concentration? Fixation on the betterment of mind, body, and soul? Certainly, all those things.

But Elizabeth and Alex taught me a lesson that day: Who said yoga has to be serious? It's just yoga, after all.

# Chapter 10

# Becoming an Older, Bolder Tortoise

*Behold the turtle.*
*He makes progress only when he sticks his neck out.*

—James Bryant Conant

E ven at 2 AM it can still be warm on a Costa Rican beach. Warm enough to wear little besides shorts, a t-shirt, and a headlamp. That's about all Kate and I had on as we slipped out of our tent and into the pitch black night. Our camp sat in a small group of trees just beyond the edge of the beach.

For a moment we both felt disoriented. The nearby sounds of feet scurrying through dry leaves did little to set our minds at ease. We suspected the noise came from the four-foot long iguanas who'd been hanging around the tent since we arrived. Still we decided it prudent to turn our headlights on to be sure that no crocodiles had made their way up from a distant river we had crossed that afternoon.

Happily, the scurrying feet *did* belong to iguanas. While not so fearsome as crocs, the iguanas still showed decidedly little respect for the boundaries of our campsite. But why should they? We had set up in their territory, after all, so I guess we couldn't really expect them to give a tongue-flicker about our desire for privacy. The myriad of white-faced monkeys that had joined us at dinnertime certainly didn't. In fact, they spent much of their visit scolding Kate and me from the trees above, then taking bites out of hard fruit and throwing them down at us. Talk about poor dinner guests!

Heading in for bed earlier in the evening, the commotion continuing about us, I had wanted to just yell out into the dark, "Would everyone *pull-eeze* just settle down out there?"

But sleep was not on the agenda, not for this night anyway. Likewise nor was a search for iguanas or crocodiles or white-faced monkeys. Instead we had pedaled down a lonely gravel road to the Pacific Ocean, then set up camp there in hopes of a late night rendezvous with a giant leatherback turtle.

Kate and I were in the midst of a month-long bicycle tour of Costa Rica. We knew little about the leatherbacks other than what we had read: that they can weigh up to 1,500 pounds and be six feet in length; that they are specially adapted for swimming in the ocean which they can do to great depths, one being recorded 4,000 feet down; and that they had been listed by the US as an endangered species since the early 1970s, with populations of nesting females in the Pacific having declined as much as 80% in more recent years. [11]

And we knew two other things:  that each year leatherbacks came onto the beach that we had camped along to lay their eggs and that egg laying season had started.  The egg laying goes on at night, presumably to protect the female leatherback from the baking sun and human predation, and to protect her eggs from the perils of marauding coyotes, birds, reptiles, crustaceans, and (you guessed it) humans.

Stepping out of the forest and onto the beach, we were hit by a sensual cornucopia:  the smell of salt; the sound of surf; the feel of a light, warm breeze; and the sight of a million stars overhead.  We headed for the water's edge to begin the first of several nights of searching.

Kate and I quickly figured out there was something ridiculously simple about searching a beach for an egg-dropping leatherback.  All you have to do is go to the surf line and start walking along it.  If you come upon a churned up track heading up onto the beach—not a little puny track but instead one looking as if a D9 Earth-Moving Cat had just emerged from the ocean—well you are half way there.

We learned to avoid the urge to immediately follow the track inland and instead to continue paralleling the surf.  If in 50 meters or so you didn't come upon another track then you had made your find:  one track signals a leatherback still on the beach, two tracks means a

---

[11] Leatherbacks live in oceans around the world.  The US listing is only one of many conservation initiatives globally designed to protect them.

leatherback already returned to the ocean.

When Kate and I found such a single giant track of churned up sand the excitement became palpable. All we needed to do was follow the track up onto the beach back toward the forest. Somewhere up there we *would* find a beast of monstrous proportions. One hundred percent guaranteed! That never happens when you see a wolf track in Yellowstone.

And oh, by the way, it's a pretty good bet that the leatherback is not going to outrun you back to the ocean.

Given the seriousness of giant turtle's business and the cathedral like feel of the night, Kate and I would pause to shut off our headlamps and take a deep breath. Then we walked quietly up the beach away from the ocean until we began to hear the steady scraping of sand and an unending series of grunts and groans.

The turtles we found were massive: my memory tells me that the biggest one was as large as a Volkswagen Beetle though surely that must be a game the mind has played on me over the years. What clearly was not a game was this massive turtle's intent to go forth and multiply, thus assuring the continuation of her species. She dug and groaned and dug and groaned and dug and groaned. With each flap of her giant front flipper sand flew in the air and the nest hole deepened.

Kate and I took up a seat on the beach, out of the turtle's line of sight and beyond the reach of the flying sand. For a long time we simply sat and watched in silence, blanketed by stars, marveling at the miracle happening before us.

After a time the leatherback stopped digging and moved into position above the giant hole she had created. In the light of a distant rising moon we could see the eggs drop one by one into the sand. Perhaps a hundred fell. Eventually she stopped and then began to arduously refill her nest, careful not to crush her eggs. She moved around the hole to assure she backfilled it deeply, but as importantly to make a massive imprint five or six times as large as the actual nest. The enormous disturbance she created would make it tougher for predators to find her eggs.

That work finally done, the giant turtle turned to make her way back to the ocean. She moved one agonizing flop forward at a time. Each time the turtle's massive flippers dropped her back to the sand she let out a tremendous groan. But the leatherback moved with such purpose that there could be no doubt she would eventually achieve her goal.

Kate and I paralleled the turtle at a respectful distance, often sitting to quietly watch and listen to her progress. After a good deal of time the leatherback made it to the edge of the surf line. She pushed into the lapping water, sticking her head far forward into the breaking surf. The next wave brought the water half way up her side. As the water receded the leatherback pushed forward another step, though this time she did not groan.

When the next wave arrived the giant turtle disappeared, reclaimed by the welcoming sea.

T he World Wildlife Fund of Australia claims that leatherback turtles live up to 150 years, maybe even longer. Possibly that's because once they reach maturity the great turtles have few natural predators other than man. If so, they probably lead a life largely free from stress, one of the many often claimed benefits of a regular yoga practice.

I don't know if anyone has ever actually tried to assess stress levels of a leatherback, but if they did they probably went straight to blood sampling to look at the turtle's cortisol levels. Cortisol is called the "stress hormone" because it is secreted in high levels during high-anxiety, fight-or-flight situations. We humans also have it coursing through our veins. Cortisol *is* necessary and positive for many life situations. However, continued and chronic stress—and the resultant elevated cortisol levels—can cause numerous negative impacts on bodily functions, including increased abdominal fat, impaired cognitive performance, and increased chance of heart attacks from elevated blood pressure.

Yoga, so they say, can help lower cortisol levels and thus help eliminate such stress-induced concerns. I don't know about you, but I'm all for something that can help me avoid being fat, dumb, and dead.

And it's apparently not all smoke and mirrors. Research by Thomas Jefferson University's Center for Integrative Medicine showed that a single, one-hour session of yoga can lower blood cortisol levels in healthy males and females with no past yoga experience. In another study, a daily hour of yoga for seven days consecutively again resulted in significantly lowered blood cortisol.

So from a stress-related standpoint, more yoga equals less stress equals less blood cortisol equals a longer life. That's one theory, anyway. Put more simply, we should all try to live like an old, mellow leatherback turtle. If we can do that maybe we can all live to be 150, too.

Yoga has always been touted as a source of long-life, claims that go way beyond the specifics of stress and cortisol. The famous Indian yogi B.K.S. Iyengar, for example, said that through our actions we can choose to put off the drought of old age:

*At a certain age the body does decay.... By performing asanas we allow the blood to nourish the extremities and the depths of the body, so that the cells remain healthy. But if you say, "No, I am old," naturally the blood circulation recedes. If the rains don't come, there is drought and famine, and if you don't do yoga—if you don't irrigate the body— then when you get drought or famine in the body as incurable diseases, you just accept them and prepare to die. Why should you allow the drought to come when you can irrigate the body?*

The irrigation analogy seems appropriate, given the way that blood carries oxygen and essential nutrition throughout the body in the same way a river is the lifeblood of a valley.

Bikram claims that healing and rejuvenating powers of Hatha yoga come from the sequential compression and release of blood to the organs, glands, and muscle groups. In an analogy paralleling Iyengar's, think of it like dam flood gates opening and closing. In theory bloodstream pressure builds up during the pose and subsequent blood release at the end of the pose results in flushing bacteria, toxins, and waste from the body, thereby leading to greater health and longer life. The US Corps of Engineers regularly puts the identical plan into place in the Grand Canyon, opening the flood gates on the Colorado River to push water up into dry arroyos, scour the streambed, redeposit sandy shorelines, and thereby revitalize the ecosystem.

Irrigation and flooding aside, just how important *can* a yoga-centered life be to staying young? Even yoga instructors can't seem to agree. Some say yes, some say no.

Ponce de León-ers can take heart because as yoga author and instructor Susan Winter Ward says,

> *Getting older doesn't have to mean getting old. We certainly don't have to accept the traditional concept that aging means declining strength, health and quality of life. We can choose to maintain and create healthy, strong, vital bodies and minds. For 5,000 years, yoga has been a path to health and living consciously in these bodies we inhabit. We're just discovering what has been known in India for thousands of years: that yoga is a personal "fountain of youth" because of its rejuvenating effects on the body and its calming influence on the mind.*

By the way, did you know that Ponce de León's search for the life giving waters of the fountain was not just because he had a desire to live to a ripe old age. No, something far more compelling. In his <u>Historia General y Natural de las Indias of 1535</u>, Gonzalo Fernández de Oviedo claimed that

Ponce de León hoped the miraculous fountain would cure his sexual impotence.  Makes sense—this was, after all, in the days before Viagra.

Another yoga instructor, Brant Rogers, takes a contrary view to Ms. Ward's "fountain of youth" claim, saying,

> Our history is strewn with the wreckage of explorers trying to find the fountain of youth. All of those doomed journeys began with the belief that we could own what we call youth. Yoga practice doesn't offer anything of the sort. It offers us a way of being whole, an opportunity to let go of the seeking for something that we can't own.

I tell you what, if the instructors can't agree, I don't know how they expect us plebeians to come to any resolution on whether yoga will help us live long like the turtle.  Regardless, I think that we all *can* get on board with the idea that aging muscles, tendons, and ligaments tend to get stiffer.  Thus anything we do to stretch them—for example yoga—will help reverse those effects.  The looser you are the more alive and young you feel.

Simple enough.

But claims to the anti-aging power of yoga go a great deal further still.  An article in *Yoga Journal* calls out 38 ways that yoga will keep you young and fit, via improvements in your sleep, circulation, lymph flow, bone density, immune system, bowel performance, and.... The list goes on to describe 32 other anti-aging benefits.  I'll spare you the details but since *Yoga Journal* has lots of knowledgeable folks who care a great deal about yoga, I feel pretty certain that they hit on most of the important benefits.

Still, comprehensive though it be, the *Yoga Journal* article did miss one anti-aging benefit of yoga. You see some of your friends out in Orange County California are now doing "facial yoga" instead of getting face lifts or having Botox treatments.

The OC. Those folks are always so far ahead of the rest of us.

F or athletes the concept of age gets a bit confused. We're all generally supposed to move through time in defined life stages: from toddler to childhood to our teens to adulthood to middle age to old age and, eventually, to senility. Along the way there is a peaking of physical prowess, then a diminishing capacity in all workings of the body. Athletes rebel against this diminishing capacity timeline, pushing the onset of old age out and out and out until, assuming they are ultimately successful, they die.

I've seen athletic prowess put off aging of the body time and time again. In my twenties and thirties, for example, I ran more than a dozen marathons. Race after race my time was so slow that it always took until the men's 70 and older age bracket before I would have earned a top-three finisher medal, had I...er...been 50 years older. And usually even then my time wouldn't have put me in first place with the septuagenarian crowd.

But interestingly enough, hardcore runners or athletes of similar persuasion don't often excel at yoga, at least not to start. Bikram claims that the worst students in his class are the world-champion athletes.

One day in class it became apparent that an incredibly fit newcomer next to me, who had earlier told me he was a marathoner, was really struggling. "You runners are always so tight," the instructor said to him, trying to move the man into a position that he rebelled against. "Come on, you need to give it a try. If you can, you must."

Later, in the locker room I asked the flushed fellow, "So how did your first class go?"

"I got totally trashed," he replied. "Totally. I'm going home for a run so I can get into some pain I understand."

The guy looked to be about 30. While many of us might be thinking about exercise and wellness by then, before 30 I don't think most of us really spend much time thinking about growing old. At least I didn't. But at 30 life begins to grow edges: the view of childhood now distant, the view of old age for the first time showing as a hint on the horizon. Approaching fifty, as I am now, brings the concept of age even more to the fore. As French writer Victor Hugo said,

*Forty is the old age of youth, fifty is the youth of old age.*

I am firmly in the crowd that believes yoga helps us retain our youth. I was once in class with an elderly woman whose tremors suggested she might be suffering from early-stage Parkinson's Disease. I watched her and marvelled at her perseverance, her strength, her youth and then later, outside of class, the vitality on her face. Another time I practiced with a young newbie to Bikrams, a fellow who could boast of 1% body fat, rippled abdominal muscles, and a birth certificate dated since the end of the Reagan presidency.   Ahead of him was an old man— probably a teen in World War II—a regular, who practiced on through the Standing Series with graceful ease while my young new friend time and again took to the floor.   The young man got run down by the yoga truck, then each time he returned to his feet the truck backed over him again.   I haven't seen that young fellow's rippled abdomen in class since.

Maybe when he hits 30.


J ust like that newbie, there is an instructor in Corvallis named John who can boast of low body fat and a sculpted physique.   But ask anyone at Elizabeth's studio and I think they'll tell you that John's outstanding feature is not his body, but instead his sense of humor. John's classes are the only ones I've ever attended where laughter can become the predominant memory of the 90 minutes, where laughter might follow practitioners out the door and into the locker room.

I had arrived at Week 8/Day 48 of my 60-day Challenge.   John paced the room like a manic comic on stage, somehow managing to instruct class while filling us in on his life's doctrine, regularly peppered with references to his mentor Bikram.   On this day the tangent John was chasing down was men and what idiots they can be. Looking up in the mirror I could see half the heads in the room regularly nodding in agreement as they chuckled.

One of those heads belonged to my sister, Suz, who

was newly attending yoga classes with me. We were standing side-by-side. Ahead of us was a man I judged to be in his 80s. The old gentleman looked slim and fit, the only sign of his age being wrinkled skin and snow white hair. Age, however, is not defined by wrinkles alone, as poet Samuel Ullman once told us:

*Nobody grows old merely by living a number of years.*
*We grow old by deserting our ideals.*
*Years may wrinkle the skin,*
*but to give up enthusiasm wrinkles the soul.*

The old man's soul clearly had no wrinkles as his enthusiasm was real. As class rolled on I soon saw that he was going far deeper into the poses than me (not that I was...er...paying attention because you are of course not supposed to be paying attention to anyone but yourself).

As John released us into *Savasana* at the end of the Standing Series, he motored on. "So it *is* true," he laughed, "that men can be good for nothing. But hey ladies, can't live with 'em, can't live without 'em, right? So don't blame us men, OK? You know what Bikram says, 'If you dig a canal and invite a crocodile into your bedroom, don't blame the crocodile when he bites your ass!'"

While John laughed unabashedly at himself, I smiled. The old man showed no outward sign of change.

Sometimes with John's numerous asides it wasn't clear when you would make it to the next pose but eventually we did move step-wise through the Sequence, arriving at *Ardha-Kurmasana*, Half Tortoise pose. The number one benefit from the pose, according to Bikram, is to help us live longer, like a tortoise.

Bringing us out of *Savasana* and then through a sit up, John said, "Ok turn around for Half Tortoise pose. Start sitting on your heels, feet together. Bring your hands up over your head, only thumbs crossed. Take a deep inhale and reach up as far as you can. Now as you exhale, suck in your stomach and bend forward slowly, back flat, body in one straight line from fingertips to the tailbone. Try to touch your head to the floor first, then your pinkies. Elbows locked; arms and wrists straight. Keep your butt to your heels—do not lift the body. This is an active pose, you should feel it in your shoulders and scapula."

I did feel it, I always do, but mostly I felt my breath and mind calming after Fixed Firm pose. We held the pose for several moments, my body relaxing, before John released us back into *Savasana*. Slow the breath, live long, be turtle-like I thought.

Just two years earlier a turtle said to be the oldest living creature on Earth had celebrated its 175th birthday. In 1835, at the ripe young age of five, "Harriet" was picked up by Charles Darwin when the *HMS Beagle* stopped at the Galapagos Islands to collect specimens. Harriet died not long ago—probably worn out I'm thinking—but most recently lived at Steve Irwin's Australia Zoo, apparently a pampered old lady who each day was given a soapy bath and a ration of her favorite treats, pink hibiscus flowers.

May we all be so lucky. Live long; be turtle-like.

During our last week in Oregon, Kate and I extended the length and frequency of our walks and visits with many wonderful friends. We spent time meandering along the beach at the coast. The pounding waves seemed to infuse Kate with strength. Day by day she looked healthier, more vibrant. Her voice strengthened. And instead of resting in bed Kate began to regularly turn on her computer and work. As a computer scientist who loves her work—name me another person who would get up at 3 AM "…just because I figured out a new way to code that problem and I was so anxious to try it I couldn't sleep!"—seeing Kate on her machine again is tantamount to an "I'm-feeling-better" sign being posted.

When Kate slept or slipped into the nerd dimension, my sister Suz and I went to yoga. It came as no surprise to me that though she was a first timer to Bikram's when we arrived in Oregon, by the end of our month Suz was making me look like the newbie. You have to understand this about Suz—she has achieved some sort of agelessness, being as slim and fit as she was in college. Her fitness comes from a lifetime of running and swimming (OK, not to mention calorie control like I have never been able to achieve). From behind in a swimming suit Suz is tough to distinguish from her two athletic teenage daughters.

I greatly admire my sister for this.

Suz's body is a testament to the possibility of the oft-repeated concept that every cell in the body replaces itself every seven years. I've heard that claim in yoga class a dozen times. We *can* stay young, they tell us, just think of it—a new body every seven years! All the evils you are perpetrating on your body today can be wiped out in just one dog year. Wow, how good does that make you feel?

I always initially get excited when I think about an entirely *new* me, yet I also always quickly fall into skepticism. Every time I hear the new-body-every-seven-years story I wonder how the heck anybody could know such a startling fact as a certainty.

So I checked.

Steve Mack, a Fellow in Molecular Biology and Cell Biology, says that he spent weeks trying to track down the origin of the new-body-every-seven-years myth. He found no primary reference, but did find that the idea has been tossed about "casually" for over 80 years, plus found one reference to it (again no data to back the claim) in a 19th century book.

But then Dr. Mack cites a 2005 paper in *Cell* that does provide some solid evidence that on average cells *may indeed* turn over every seven years. In the paper Spalding and co-researchers report using levels of the carbon-14 isotope for their testing. Why carbon-14? Levels of carbon-14 spiked in the atmosphere during above ground nuclear bomb testing prior to 1963. That carbon-14 eventually joined the food chain and from there came into our bodies via the plants and animals we have eaten.

OK, so how do we get from that point to knowing how old our cells are? Simple, grasshopper. By knowing two facts: 1) that cellular levels of carbon-14 reflect atmospheric levels of carbon-14 at the time the cells are formed, and 2) that genomic DNA is not exchanged after a cell has gone through its last division. (Come on, you knew all that, right?)  Oh those things *and* a little math wizardry, and a big black top hat that you tap three times with a baton.

Kazaam!

Out of the top hat pops an interesting result:  different cells have different lifetimes.  Red blood cells last roughly 120 days, skin cells 14 days, the cells on the surface of the gut five days, the rest of the gut almost 16 years, skeletal muscle 15 years.  Then there are the brain and heart, which appear to have limited or no ability to replace their supply of cells.  So no, we do not get an *entirely* new body every seven years, but *on average* you might be able to make a case that our cells turn over at somewhere in that time period.

But forget the new-body-every-seven-years concept. What really intrigues me out of this line of research is the idea that the heart and mind cannot generate replacement cells.  Just think of that:  when it comes to the heart and mind we get what we get, period.  Just one more reason it's imperative that we keep our hearts and minds ever healthy and ever open.

# Good Camel, Good Rabbit

*I believe that the very purpose of our life is to seek happiness.*

—Dalai Lama

We arrived home a couple of days ago, having made the long drive back from Oregon. And we are good at this moment. Kate continues her steady recovery. Our time in Portland is done and we are happy to be home with friends, and with Kate's personal healing agent, our cat Tigger.

It is nice to sleep in our own bed.

While Kate cross country skis with our friend Lu somewhere out in the nearby mountains, I head back to Chris and Rebekah's studio. Week 9/Day 53; seven days of my 60-day Challenge left. I am pleased to see that Meg, a visiting instructor from Missoula, is teaching. Meg is Italian to the core, from her "...anzio" last name to her beautiful flowing black hair to the hand waving motions she makes as she talks. She also is one of the most inspiring teachers I've ever taken a class from, yoga or otherwise.

Why?   For a single reason: passion—passion for her students, passion for the yoga.

We have just completed Half Tortoise pose and are heading into *Savasana*.  Meg has a way of snapping her fingers three times and saying "Three, two, one…you should be in *Savasana* already, gathering the benefits" that demands attention.  "No dallying," she continues.  "No adjusting the costume.  No need to wipe off the sweat—it's there to cool you so wiping it off will just make you hotter anyway.  Just soften your gaze, be still, and breathe in *Savasana*.  Eventually you should only need to take one breathe for the entire 20 seconds."

We rest and I stare blankly at the ceiling, having a hard time holding back the giddiness I feel about soon completing the Challenge. I feel different, stronger, more at ease, less stressed. Is it the yoga? I think so but in truth I also realize that my psyche and outlook are always a reflection of my concerns for Kate. When she feels well, I feel well.

Meg stands up to adjust the heat in the room.  As she walks to thermostat she says, "The final four poses are the deepest back stretches of class.  We work the spine in all four directions."

We complete a sit up then move on to the pose that in my early Bikram days nearly caused me to black out several times.  "Come to the top of your mat," Meg says, "for *Ustrasana*, Camel pose.  Kneeling position, knees and feet six inches apart.  This is the deepest back bend that we do; *everything* we have done to this point in class has been in preparation for this pose."

Under Meg's instruction we put our hands to our hips, then drop our heads back, looking for the brick wall behind us. Next we reach back with first the right hand, then the left, each hand grabbing the heel of the corresponding  foot, arching our backs dramatically. "Now push your stomach, hips, and thighs far forward," Meg urges us. "Don't rest on your hands—instead your hands should hold you in place. You should be pushing forward so hard that if you let go you would fly forward."

There are a couple of first timers in class who don't know what they've signed up for here, but they quickly learn—groaning audibly one of the newbies behind me comes out of the pose, dropping her head to the floor. The other also soon falls. Meg verifies what they've already begun to discover, "For you first timers it is completely normal to feel a whole range of sensations during this pose: elation, ecstasy, pain, dizziness, nausea. The good news is that all of those things are normal and good for you. You're opening up your chest, opening your throat and heart chakras, exposing yourself in a way that may feel unnatural but is so good for your spine, counteracting the slouching, stooping, and chair sitting we do every day."

"You may even see stars," Meg continues. "Don't worry, there's no extra charge."

I've never quite understood where the "camel" in camel pose comes from. It looks more like a box to me, but perhaps the extended chest is supposed to evoke the camel's hump.

As a kid I think we all learn that the camel's hump exists to store water. But in case you fell asleep in ninth grade biology class, this bulletin just in: the hump is made of fat, not filled with water. The camel can go weeks (and depending on conditions, possibly months) without eating, pulling energy from the hump until the hump is so depleted that it can droop over like a deflated balloon until replenished.

Even though the hump[12] does not store water, camels do have prodigious abilities to store water allowing them to withstand long periods of time without fluid intake. They can drink up to 150 L (roughly 40 gal) in single sitting. The ability to gorge on and store water that way is clearly useful if you plan to live your life in the desert, where you might travel days on end between watering holes. But 40 gallons? That's a lot of water—330 pounds to be exact— some 20% of mature animal's weight!

Just imagine what suddenly *gaining* 20% of your body weight in water would do to you. I can't even drink down a liter of water in yoga class without feeling immediately sick. What I can do in class is sweat, a lot. A camel, of course, has no interest in sweating all that water back out. In fact, given the desiccating power of the desert camels are fully adapted to hold on tightly to every last drop.

Let's consider the concept of *sweating out* 20% of your body weight in water. If you were to drop that amount of

---

[12] Actually, saying "hump" is to ignore that there are two kinds of camels. The dromedary has a single hump; the Bactrian has two humps.

water without replenishment you would die, but not
before first passing through several unpleasantries such as
massive headaches, dizziness, nausea, delirium, and coma.
But when a camel becomes dehydrated, its kidneys are
capable of producing extremely concentrated urine,
thereby retaining water and thus helping maintain blood
viscosity and pressure levels near normal.[13] Likewise, a
camel's red blood cells are oval (ours are round) to better
facilitate blood flow during periods of dehydration. A
camel's nose even has the ability to re-absorb water vapor
from the air it is breathing out.

Of all the camel thermoregulatory adaptations,
however, I want the one that allows them to uniquely live
through great fluctuations in core body temperature (from
93 °F at night to 106 °F in the day by one estimate).
Camels can live through those fluctuations while still
maintaining the full repertoire of metabolic reactions
needed for life. And they don't even *start* to sweat until
they hit the upper end of the temperature range. Bikram
Yoga classes are typically 105 °F so a camel would fare just
fine should we be able to smuggle it into the hot studio. I
think being camel-like and having my body temperature
drift up to 106 °F without even breaking a sweat would be
quite nice on those days when I'm becoming dizzy and
nauseated in Camel pose.

But there's something that goes along with all that
sweaty heat, too. Oxygen deprivation. One day a few

---

[13] Even with that unique ability normal kidney function has been found to
return to an extremely dehydrated camel within 30 minutes of drinking.

years ago—back when I regularly nearly passed out during Camel—I went through two sets of the pose calculating whether the volume of air in the tightly closed up studio was sufficient to sustain 35 deep-breathing people.    I estimated the volume of a human lung, the volume of air in the room, the concentration of oxygen in the air, the number of respirations per person per minute, the .... (I know, you can go ahead and say it—it's little wonder nobody gathers around engineers for stimulating conversation at cocktail parties!) By the end of the second set of Camel I had come to the conclusion that no, indeed, there was not enough air in the room and we should all be dead.

That's when I collapsed on the floor a second time.

After class I told Rebekah about my concern, about how my calculations showed that none of us should be alive.  She chuckled and rolled her eyes, saying, "Actually, we bring in air from outside through the heater, so there should be plenty of oxygen.  I think everyone will be just fine."

Another great theory destroyed by the facts.

After Meg runs us through the second set of Camel, we move on to Rabbit pose.  She starts us sitting on our knees, Japanese style, then has us reach back and wrap our towel over our heels and grab on tightly.  "Now," she says, "round over, bringing your chin to your chest and look at your belly button.  As you exhale curl your torso forward, bringing your head to the floor, forehead touching your knees.  Once your head is on the

floor do not move it; this is to
protect your neck. Keep looking at
your stomach and pull on your heels
with all your strength, arms
straight, heels together, feet flat on
the floor, thighs lifting up to
perpendicular to the floor."

Now this one I get; surely in the final expression of the
Rabbit pose I can see myself as a bunny sitting in the grass.
And for once—at least aside from waiting for rescue in a
snowbound, broken down car—having too big a stomach
comes in handy. As it spills out onto my thighs I can easily
stare at my belly button, no problem-o. Yes, nine weeks
into the Challenge and my stomach is still there. Firmer,
surely. At least I want to think so. But if you're the kind
that worries about such things, let me get it over with right
now. One week from the end of my Challenge I cannot in
good faith tell you that I have lost the 15 pounds I wanted
to lose. Maybe two pounds.

Maybe.

Meg carries on, standing right beside me, as I continue
to gaze at my belly button. "Rabbit is the perfect
complement to Camel, undoing the tremendous spinal
compression by stretching out each and every vertebrate
like pearl necklace on an elastic string." She tells the story
that I have heard often, that in teacher training they
measure the difference in spine length between Rabbit and
Camel and find the spine can compress or extend twelve
inches or more—you can actually measure that difference
on a single person between the two poses. My mind drifts

for a moment, remembering that elsewhere I have also heard that some yogis believe that a person's age is determined by the flexibility of his or her spine, not by their chronological age. It takes only a single trip through any retirement home in the world to make that idea not seem daft.

Meg's voice pulls me back: "These two poses, Camel and Rabbit, are tremendous for your nervous system, for your neck and spine, helping alleviate backaches and sore back muscles, increasing mobility. As Bikram always says, 'Good spine, good life'."

When Meg brings us out of Rabbit I feel strong, relaxed, at peace. Two poses and a breathing exercise left. At this point I always know that I will make it through class. Camel and Rabbit are the last two places I feel any consternation. Sometimes, as on this day, I spend an extra second looking into my eyes in the mirror—an early celebration of sorts—before dropping into *Savasana*.

I feel pleased.

And nine weeks into the Challenge, with Kate out on her skis somewhere in the mountains, I also feel happy. "Good spine, good life"? Yes, I think now gazing at the ceiling, but even better I like a corollary to Bikram's saying: "Good camel, good rabbit, good life."

A friend of mine recently visited the ancient city of Dunhuang in northwestern China. He talked of seeing interesting figures in the museum and in the nearby Mogao Caves. One symbol showed three rabbits chasing each other in a never-ending circle sort of akin to the ubiquitous chasing-arrow recycle symbol. The figure, placed in the caves by Buddhist monks, is odd because each rabbit shares one ear with one of the other rabbits,  meaning three ears suffice to suggest six ears.

Guan Youhui, a retired researcher from the Dunhuang Academy, spent 50 years studying such decorative patterns as those in the Mogao Caves. He believes the three-rabbit image came to Dunhuang indirectly from the West by way of Central China. He bases his theory on knowledge that Dunhuang was an important stop on the Silk Road dating back to the Han dynasty (206 BC to 220 AD). Mr. Youhui has interpreted the symbol this way: "The rabbits—like many images in Chinese folk art that carry auspicious symbolism—represent peace and tranquility."

A similar chasing rabbit symbol has also been found in present day Tibet. I have to wonder if today's Tibetans would go along with the idea of the Chinese symbol as being auspicious—i.e., attended by favorable circumstances—or as representative of peace or tranquility.

Not long ago the pre-Olympic Olympic torch relay from Greece to China was underway in preparation for the XXIX Olympiad, to be held in Beijing. Here is another symbol, the five interlocked rings representing, according to the International Olympic Committee, the international nature of the Olympic movement and the fact that all nations of the world are welcome.

That is, of course, if you can get yourself recognized as

a nation.  To wit, the Olympic torch relay attracted thousands of protestors across the world who sought to focus world attention, among myriad issues, on the people of Tibet's right to autonomy, independence, and self-determination.  On separate occasions the Dalai Lama, who has been Tibet's spiritual leader in exile since 1959, has captured the protesters' sentiments this way:

> *The new Chinese settlers have created an alternate society: a Chinese apartheid which, denying Tibetans equal social and economic status in our own land, threatens to finally overwhelm and absorb us. ... Whether intentionally or unintentionally, some kind of cultural genocide is taking place.*

The genocide and oppression are taking place on many levels, from suppressing the Tibetan language, to tearing down traditional Buddhist monasteries, to an enforced requirement that monks denounce the exiled Dalai Lama.  In the lead up to the Olympics the Chinese killed dozens of Buddhist monks and others protesting on the anniversary of the failed 1959 rebellion against forced Chinese rule.

Importantly, although Tibet's Communist Party secretary called him "a jackal in Buddhist monk's robes" the Dalai Lama has urged non-violence, saying that it is "...futile and not helpful to create hate in the hearts of Chinese people".  The Dalai Lama has stated that he does not necessarily want independence from China, and that the Tibetan people are not anti-Chinese.  They even supported the Olympic Games.  He just wants greater autonomy for his homeland.

To think that it could have all been different, led by

Olympics, led by the Olympic torch relay which traveled onto the Tibetan Plateau and through Dunhuang. At Dunhuang the two symbols so far separated in time—the Olympic torch and the chasing rabbits—must have met ever so briefly. The Chinese and Tibetans could have arrived together at the point of auspicious symbolism for peace and tranquility that the rabbits represent. Perhaps at a ceremony to return autonomy to the Tibetan people, someone could have read the Olympic Creed, which says,

> *The most important thing in the Olympic Games is not to win but to take part, just as the most important thing in life is not the triumph but the struggle.*

And then perhaps they could have turned to the Dalai Lama, who understands along with all Tibetans what it is to struggle without triumph. Perhaps he would have looked out at the Chinese and Tibetans gathered about, then reprised the words he spoke at his 1989 Nobel Peace Prize acceptance ceremony:

> *Ours has been a long struggle. We know our cause is just because violence can only breed more violence and suffering, our struggle must remain non-violent and free of hatred. We are trying to end the suffering of our people, not to inflict suffering upon others.*

This great event did not occur when the Olympic torch passed through Dunhuang and crossed paths with the symbol of the rabbits, but perhaps it might still come to pass in the years ahead.

Perhaps.

# Chapter 12

# Thankfulness

*You simply will not be the same person two months from now
after consciously giving thanks each day
for the abundance that exists in your life.*

—Sarah Ban Breathnach

K ate and I are sitting in church with my folks in Billings, 140 miles from our home in Bozeman. The regular minister, Tim Hathaway, is not preaching and I am disappointed because I never leave a sermon of his without feeling thankful for some bit of enlightenment, without feeling that I've been given something important to ponder through the day.  Instead on this Sunday morning there is a visiting pastor from Shepherd, a small town outside of Billings.

The visiting minister speaks of faith in God, of the age-old conundrum of believing in something that you cannot see or feel or quantify.  His testimony is powerful, and he speaks of his gratitude for many times being able to witness faith in action, either from something happening directly to him or through the good acts of people around him.  His concluding remarks about believing in God are simple, "You can never know for sure—that's why they call it 'faith'."

W e are back in Bozeman now as I make ready for the second-to-the-last class of my 60-day Challenge, the second-to-the-last-day of two straight months of yoga.  Week 10/Day 59.

I am looking forward to class here at the end as much as always; my enthusiasm hasn't diminished at all over the ten weeks.  Even if I am tired or down, I continue to know that by the end of each class I will feel reenergized and refocused.  So lack of enthusiasm is not a concern.

I have, however, spent a stupid amount of time this week trying to decide if I should go six days straight in my tenth week, do a double on my last day, have a rest day before day 60, and so on.  And then I began to fret that I would have a mishap on the way to the yoga studio—my bike tire going flat, or the battery on our motor scooter going dead, or getting in a car accident—which causes me to miss class that day.  So in that last week I started to go to the first class of the day to be sure I will have a second chance lest something goes awry.

It's silly, I know, but I so want a clean completion of this effort, an effort that felt so monumental to start, still does, but now I know I can finish and I just don't want to mess it up because something asinine happens.

Writer Barbara Kingsolver once wrote, "Personal quests do have a way of taking on lives of their own, even when nobody else knows or cares." In truth no one really does care if I finish the Challenge but me … and Kate … and likely Chris and Rebekah, and possibly Wendy and Elizabeth and my sister Suz. But that's about it. Ok, and maybe also that green, somewhat slimy purveyor of wisdom Kermit the Frog, who said,

> *Life's like a movie, write your own ending*
> *Keep believing, keep pretending*
> *We've done just what we set out to do….*

I *do* want to write my own ending. In it, I want one thing above all to be at the fore. Not the number of days or the endless sweat or the sore hamstrings or the weight loss (OK, true, there wasn't much of that). What I want to take away from the end of my Challenge is a sense of overwhelming thankfulness, for it is only in a spirit of thankfulness that achievement matters.

More and more as I approach Day 60, I feel truly thankful and blessed for the health and time even to dream to attempt, much less complete, such a monumental effort to improve the body, mind, and spirit.

On that second-to-the-last day of class I show up 30 minutes early. I *never* do that. I plant myself in the studio so I am certain that barring a tsunami—and that doesn't happen very often in Bozeman—Week 10/Day 59 will be in the bag. Rebekah is teaching and we have pushed through the Standing Series and well into the Floor Series.

As has happened in many classes in Corvallis and here in Bozeman over the last few weeks, Rebekah mentions to the class that I am near the end of my Bikram Challenge. She also mentions that two other students are just starting Challenges, and encourages others to consider a Challenge of their own.

"Sorry, what is this Challenge you're talking about?" a first timer to class asks.

Lying there in *Savasana*, the question gives me momentary pause, but not Rebekah, who answers immediately, "The Challenge is a way to help you see your potential, which is limitless."

Rebekah has worked us for 85 minutes up to Head to Knee, a pose that looks ever so much like a runner's stretch, done on both sides. When we complete the second side she says, "Now lie down, and do a quick sit up, double exhale, both legs straight out in front of you. Make a peace sign out of your two fingers and karate chop between the big and next toe on each foot. Now grab hold of your big toes as if your fingers were two big meat hooks. Move your hips back and forth five, ten times to get on the sits-bones. Lock the knees, lift your feet off the ground, and *if you can* lower your chest and stomach to your thighs. Eventually—maybe today, maybe someday in the future—your  destination is to touch your forehead to your knees. But until then keep back flat, chin up looking into the mirror."

I struggle simply to keep my legs locked and have little ability to lean forward or lift my feet off the ground. This sad state of affairs has not changed dramatically in the last ten weeks. For this two-legged portion of the pose I have heard that at teacher training Bikram gives a special award to any man who can put his chest on his thighs. My guess is that Bikram's awards stash never runs short of supply.

While we rest in *Savasana* Rebekah talks as she circles the room, heading back for the instructor's podium. "For our first timer," she says, "great job to make it to this point, only 17 more postures to go." There is a groan from the newbie, and laughter from everyone else. Instructors love this gag.

"No seriously," Rebekah continues, a smile in her voice, "one more pose and final breathing and we're done. You've nearly made it so stay focused and finish strong."

She has us do a sit up, then says, "You've been preparing the entire class for this moment, so make it good. *Ardha-Matsyendrasana*, Spine-Twisting pose. Everyone turn to face the brick wall. Bring your right foot under your left thigh, knee bent, right heel touching the left hip. Now bring the left leg over top, left heel just to the outside of the right knee. Then bring your right arm out and over the left knee, reaching down to grab your right knee. If you can't grab your right knee, grab the towel."

I have managed to grab my knee once in 58 days so far, and today does not make it twice in 59. I grab the towel.

"Now keeping your spine straight bring your left hand behind your back, touching the floor if you need to for

balance but eventually in the future working your arm all
the way around your body until you can grab your right
thigh.  Now exhale and twist.  Look for the mirror all the
way around behind you.  Breathe in...exhale...and twist."

I don't grab the right thigh but instead reach out to the
ground as far around my body as I can.  I do manage to
catch a glimpse of myself in the mirror and it is just then,
59 days into the Challenge, bathed in sweat, that I realize
that all I need is for someone to spread a little mustard on
me and I truly will have achieved yoga nirvana:  I will have
become a pretzel.

A hot, ever-so-salty pretzel.


N irvana is one of those words that leaves many
people feeling happy, yet perhaps also a little bit
uncomfortable, especially if you come from a Judeo-
Christian background like myself.  I think the discomfort
comes from not really knowing just what nirvana means,
for it having sort of a New Age-y, eastern religion, they-
don't-even-believe-in-God-do-they sort of connotation.

According to the Supreme Buddha[14], the word
"nirvana" describes perfect peace of mind, a place of
enlightenment and liberation from anger or longing.  In the
Jaina Sutras, the Supreme Buddha says, "There is a safe
place in view of all, but difficult of approach, where there is

---

[14] Siddhārtha Gautama, the founder of Buddhism, is generally recognized
as the Supreme Buddha of our age.  He lived sometime around 400 or
500 BC in a region called Kapilavastu, thought to be made up of parts of
today's Nepal and India.

no old age nor death, no pain nor disease. It is what is called Nirvana...."

That sounds a lot like what I've always been told is a place called *heaven*.

Like the word nirvana, the concept of yoga can leave some people a little cold. Some people seem to think that yoga *is* a religion. But if you're in that camp I ask you this: How many times has anyone ever tried to convert you to yoga? How many wars have you ever heard of carried out in the name of yoga? People killed in the name of yoga? Enough said.

But yoga can, and in many people does, engender spirituality. I think that's where the confusion comes in because somewhere in here there is a cross-over point, between religion and spirituality that is. Indeed Bikram has said that yoga *is not* religion but it *is* spirituality:

*Yoga provides us with positive, useful tools to help us realize the God within us and achieve real liberation and perfection of the soul. That is not religion, but rather Spirituality. Spirit is the expression of God through the medium of our human body.*

Religion and spirituality are clearly related words, but also strangely divergent. I think that someone can be spiritual but not religious, or religious but not spiritual. Being both is surely possible, but in my experience with many (most?) people you get one, the other, or none.

For better or worse, being religious these days has often become synonymous, sadly, with intolerance for your neighbor's beliefs. Here I am not thinking of my personal, church-going experiences which have been mostly highly positive. Instead I am thinking more broadly of the anger and terrible behaviors religion can produce in some: killing in the name of a God you purport to believe in, using religion as a justification for forcing teenage girls into polygamous relationships, intolerance between faiths and even within sects of a given faith, wars over spiritual beliefs and sacred ground, unbridled genocide, terrorism, and more.

Being spiritual, on the contrary, has most often become synonymous with having compassion for your fellow man. Being spiritual means being mindful of people *and* the world around us and working for their betterment. And being spiritual means being thankful. Body, mind, soul—I am thankful that the practice of yoga helps me to improve each of these aspects of my life, thereby making me a better person.

I think Meister Eckhart's—a German theologian, philosopher, and mystic of the Middle Ages—observation on the whole religion/spirituality question might just cover the situation the best:

*If the only prayer you said in your whole life was,*
*"Thank you," that would suffice.*

Such is the spirit of gratitude I seek to carry with me each day.


**W**eek 10/Day 60. The last day of my 60-day Challenge. I am driving, listening to National Public Radio, and they are interviewing a man about

American football. A seemingly unremarkable story, except that the man happens to be an Australian who moved his entire family, his entire life, and his charming accent half way around the world to fulfill his dream of spending a season watching the Green Bay Packers of the National Football League.

The interviewer struggles, without much success, to pull the quirky meaning of it all from the crazed Packer fan from Down Under. I think they talk about rugby and cricket and kangaroos. Maybe wombats. Nothing really strikes the mark about why this man has uprooted his life to come to the Cheese-Head state of Wisconsin. Then toward the end of the piece the Aussie finally captures the essence of his story for the hapless interviewer, saying, "Look, a man without a dream will never have a dream come true."

I smile, happy in the wisdom of the Aussie's comment, happy that I am parking the car 30 minutes before class, happy in the realization that barring a slip on the ice between the car and the building I *will* complete my Challenge.

I think that completion, just like the pathway or the process, is important. Completion validates having dreams. Completion gives us power to believe that we can achieve anything we can imagine. We should be thankful for every act of completion.

When I walk into the studio it is a Saturday morning, 730 AM. I have come for this early class since if I miss it I will have another shot at 4 PM that afternoon. Jessie, a new instructor freshly back from Bikram's teacher training, is sitting behind the desk signing folks in. We have never met, though I knew that she had been in at teacher training with Even and the instructor trainees I met in Corvallis. This is only Jessie's second week as an instructor and probably third or fourth time teaching. Chris is also there, helping Jessie with the computer, helping her get everything set up for class.

Chris gives me a great big smile. He is dressed in ski gear and says he is on his way out for the day into the nearby mountains. He knows that today is my final day of the Challenge. I get the strongest feeling that he came in that morning to congratulate me, and that the drop in to help Jessie is just a ruse to get him to the studio. This may be total fanciful thinking on my part. But still when he introduces me and then tells Jessie about this being my big finishing day of the Challenge I am sure I can hear pride in his voice.

It makes me feel really good.

Just before I go into the studio, Chris hugs me, him in bulky winter clothes, me in shorts and nothing else. Chris says, "Congratulations my friend, I wish I could be in there with you."

Chris heads for the door and I turn to enter the empty studio. In that moment I feel so thankful for Chris and Rebekah, for the community they have created, for the help that the yoga has given me over the hard months of Kate's health difficulties. Namaste my friends, I think, I honor the goodness, the Godliness, in you.

That final day of class, Day 60, is in truth anti-climatic. For a celebratory day it turns out to be a small class and one where for once I don't know that many folks. That matters not, of course; as each pose comes to completion I smile and feel gratitude for the great countdown to the end of my Challenge. I know that even if I get hit by the yoga truck—and I don't plan on that happening—that I am in the room and that's what matters. I will finish.

Jessie glides through the class smoothly, though with a beginning teacher's tendency to stay anchored at the front of the room, to stick directly to the Dialogue, and to avoid using anyone's name. I hear Jessie use many Bikram-isms that I suspect come straight out of her recent months of training. In Half Moon pose she tells us to stretch "left and right and left and right" in a peculiar staccato that almost all instructors use, apparently mimicking Bikram's rhythm. She tells us we should work with "gravitation" in Camel and urges us to "go up much more higher" in Lotus. Though it's pretty clear already, when Jessie urges us to display "English Bulldog determination and Bengal Tiger strength" I am finally, unalterably convinced that my suspicions are true—she has been Bikram-ized!

By the time Jessie works us through the Sequence and heads us back into *Savasana* after Spine-Twisting pose, I am sweaty and flushed and exceedingly happy. "Congratulations, you've made it," Jessie says. "Just a single breathing exercise left." She has us do our final sit up, then continues, "Turnaround and come to anywhere on your mat for *Kapalbhati*, Breath of Fire, the final breathing exercise. We begin with a breathing exercise; we end with a breathing exercise. Kneel in Japanese position, sitting on your feet with your hands on your knees, back straight, elbows locked."

I position myself just so, always enjoying this moment to stare into the mirror, into my own eyes. Sometimes what I see there seems empty; sometimes so much more. Today what I see is a life filled with endless possibilities. I cannot help but once again smile and feel grateful.

When I started the 60-day Challenge I did not know for certain that I would or could complete it; my weak body or mind and Kate's health all had the power to end the quest. But we did have faith. Faith allowed us to dream. Faith allowed us to start into our next challenge. "You can never know for sure," the minister had said. "That's why they call it 'faith'."

Jessie continues. "Mouth open, pursed lips, snap in your belly with each exhale as if you were blowing out a candle six feet in front of you. Don't worry about the inhale, that will come naturally. Just stay with me...and begin." She starts to clap in a slow,  steady rhythm. I breathe, we all do, and I look into the mirror.

After the first set winds down we pause a moment, then do another, this time more rapidly. I purse my lips and snap my stomach to exhale in time with Jessie's clapping. When she finishes the set she says, "Pause for a moment to congratulate yourself, to acknowledge your hard work. You've completed your maintenance for the day. Now have a drink, then turn around and lie down in final *Savasana*." Jessie walks to the door and dims the lights before continuing. "Stay at least a couple of minutes to gather the full benefit of the gift you've given yourself this morning. It has been my pleasure to teach you. Thank you for sharing your energy with me. Namaste."

I don't turn around right away but instead look into the mirror and smile. A single drop of sweat rolls down my forehead, then out onto the tip of my nose before it falls to my drenched towel.

When I exit the studio Jessie greets me, and with a beautiful smile and great enthusiasm hugs me in congratulations. Her selfless expression of joy for me—someone she did not even know 90 minutes earlier—makes me incredibly happy.

It is my second congratulatory hug of the day and it feels ever so good.

After my shower, Day 60 and the Challenge officially complete, I head downstairs to wait for Kate to pick me up. She picked up the car to go to an appointment and I know she will be late to get me. I sit on the stairway, pushing my wet gym bag aside so others can pass. I take a drink of cold water, and for the sixtieth day in the last seventy am aware of my body's post-class afterglow.

A classmate taps me on the shoulder as he passes and says, "Congratulations. I've always wondered if I could do the Challenge."

I smile and say a sincere "Thanks," then add, "I'm sure you would do just fine. You should try it, that's the only way you'll find out."

Later, when most everyone has left, I sit alone and

stare out the window, thinking. I am happy beyond reason and feel silly to see myself smiling in the reflection of the glass. Why am I smiling? Because by completing the Challenge I recognize that I have crossed into a new level of self realization. I don't mean that in some mysterious, you-could-never-do-this-without-contemplating-your-belly-button-for-a-year sort of way. No, instead what I feel at that moment is something much simpler, more akin to new confidence in myself.

That confidence comes on many levels. I am stronger physically, no doubt, something I see reflected in the strength of my core. I see my ribs more often these days, and sometimes even the outline of my abdominal muscles. More importantly my posture has improved. A new strength radiates from my back and spine; I know it's there every time I choose to sit in a straight back chair because slouching no longer feels right.

But there's something even more important. I gain strength from knowing that if in the future I ever find myself physically downtrodden or sick I could employ another Challenge as a way to bring my body back to well being.

I am stronger mentally, particularly from the discipline imposed by the practice. I think that one could do the Challenge without accepting the discipline Bikram seeks to impose: staying present, not fidgeting or wiping the sweat, focusing on your own eyes in the mirror, ignoring the pain or discomfort caused by holding a pose, not worrying about what anyone else in class is doing, making a sincere effort to do each posture the right way even when that can prove so tough. Yes, you could probably complete the Challenge without such discipline, but I think you would lose one of the big things, mental strength, that the Challenge offers as a reward.

In the same way, perhaps one could achieve the same growth—the confidence I am speaking about—without going through the Challenge but instead by simply practicing regularly for years, say twice a week. I don't know…maybe. But a commitment to the Challenge forces you to say, "This is what I am doing, this is my focus, this effort will be core to my being for ten weeks." I think such a commitment opens you to an entirely new set of possibilities for your body, mind, and soul.

My improved mental strength has manifested in a number of ways outside of class. First, the knowledge that I had the discipline to get into class each and every day bolsters me when I encounter real life demands that require my long-term commitment. Second, the Challenge helped me build mental strength to support a long-time goal of living in the present moment. I really needed to be able to focus on day 17 without worrying that 43 more days were still to come and oh boy didn't that seem like a whole lot. Let's get through today, I often told myself, I can worry about getting through tomorrow's class tomorrow.

The Challenge also gave me the mental strength to deal with the stress I felt from Kate's health challenges. I was better for her because each day in class I could let go of my mental strife, even if just for 90 minutes, and then return to her being more centered, having greater capacity to help and care and love. I think that relief of stress will be a key memory I take away from the Challenge. I now feel I have a tool—the Challenge yes but also yoga more broadly—to help me deal with life's stressful times. Knowing I have that tool in my pocket is a great confidence builder.

I think along with stress relief the Challenge taught me about achieving spiritual peace. Strange, but the simple act of breathing can bring a sense of peace and control when life presents only fear and chaos. I appreciate so much now Bikram's statements about not allowing anyone or anything steal our peace. Almost daily that thought echoes in my mind when I find myself slipping into anger over small things.

My spirit has also been enriched by the community developed through the Challenge. I should say "communities", given all the moving between studios I did as we moved for Kate's health care. I found community across three studios with hundreds of students all based on our shared experience in the Torture Chamber. Community is important to me because I love people. Everyone has a story and a talent and a purpose but so often we don't recognize this wonder, instead we just look right through each other.

Finally, I found that sweating in a small hot room with lots of half dressed people cuts through many of the false walls we erect between ourselves. I had to be open to those interactions, true. But the confidence that built through the Challenge enabled me to set aside petty doubts to become open to the possibilities existing not only in myself, but in others, as well.

H appy as I am as I wait for Kate, seeing that silly grin reflected in the window, something is still nagging at me and it takes a few moments to figure out what it is. Finally I hit on it. "Congratulate yourself," Jessie had said. "You've completed your maintenance for the day."

That's what feels odd.

Zeroing in, I realize that the phrase *maintenance for the day* is what has unsettled me. Staring at the gym bag filled with wet gear at my feet, it suddenly becomes clear that in the big scheme of things my completion of the 60-day Challenge is really just a small step in a life-long process. Completing the Challenge today is a big deal to me, no doubt, but in truth today I was simply a single person of many working for the betterment of his body, mind, and soul. Two months from now the knowledge that I completed my Challenge will continue to bolster my confidence, surely, but I still need to practice yoga if I am to derive continuing benefits from it. Yoga is not an ends to a means but rather a means to an end, that end being wellness of body, mind, and soul. This realization is somehow at once sobering and liberating.

Bikram says that he is regularly asked by students how often they must practice. His answer is simple and to the point:

*Well, how often do you plan to use your body? ... I'm guessing that you pretty much use it daily.... So you must practice your Hatha Yoga every day.*

In the locker room one day after class I heard that

message more intimately from an old man I had practiced with for many days. Marveling at his enthusiasm and ability, I boldly asked him how old he was.

"Eighty-two years old," he told me.

"Wow, how long have you been doing Bikram Yoga?" I asked.

"Twenty-eight years." His responses were brief, signaling no desire for conversation, but not knowing when to quit, I plowed on.

"That's amazing!" I said. "You are in such great condition. Do you have any words of wisdom for me?" I would love to tell you that's not what I said, but it is, so there you have it.

The old gentleman looked at me a bit askance, as if to say you sure are a queer bird, then brushed his white hair off his sweating brow. He paused and looked down as if really thinking. There was a momentary silence, then he looked up and said, "Keep coming. Always. Even if it's only once a week. That's the secret."

And so even as I see Kate pull up to the door on that final day of my 60-day Challenge, I am realizing that this is not an end, but instead a beginning. Completion helps us believe in dreams, yes, but it also signifies a point of transition—to the next dream, to the next new start, to the next challenge.

I climb into the car and with a big smile Kate says, "Hooray, you made it! I am *so* proud of you! So how did it go?"

I don't answer but instead I hug her, not letting go, and it is the best hug of the day.

# AFTER

# Epilogue

## Breathe, Sweat, Prosper

What is life?
It is the flash of a firefly in the night.
It is the breath of a buffalo in the wintertime.
It is the little shadow which runs across the grass
and loses itself in the sunset.

—Crowfoot

W eeks have passed since the completion of my 60-Day Challenge. I've been back to the studio many times, settling in on a two-day-a-week schedule, twice as much as I generally went before the Challenge.

On one of the days back I took class from Wendy, she of flowing auburn hair, rosy cheeks, and part-time Carolina southern drawl. Wendy had been a big supporter along the way, but I haven't seen her for a while as she had been travelling during weeks nine and ten of my Challenge, plus I had been gone before that for the month in Oregon. On that first class back with Wendy, she gave me a big congratulatory hug out front of the studio.

It was a huge class that day, bursting at the seams, and Wendy mentioned the completion of my Challenge a couple of times, embarrassing me surely but also giving me a sense of pride.   Then at the end of the first round Balancing Stick she said, "Scott come up here.  I want you to demonstrate because some people just aren't getting it. You are."

"Me?" I said incredulously.  Understand that it is rare for an instructor to give a demonstration, almost unheard of for a student to be called upon.

"You."  Wendy had a mischievous smile on her face.

Seventy eyeballs followed the chubby guy to the front of the room.   Thankfully Wendy gave me some clues about what I was doing right so I didn't embarrass myself.  She talked me through the pose, saying, "See how he keeps his head up (I discretely raise my head) and his back foot pointed (I quickly point my foot)."  Thankfully I didn't fall. She said thanks and 70 hands came together for a brief moment of clapping.   I stepped back to my mat, embarrassed, but grateful for the kindness that Wendy and my fellow classmates have extended me.

At the end of class that day as we lay in final *Savasana,* Wendy said, "I promised myself that if you had energy today, if you inspired me today, that I would sing a song for you.  Well whoo-ee, you folks were awesome today!  So I will sing."

This in my experience was a never-been-done moment made all the more special by the beautiful, robust voice that Wendy rocked the room with:

*I have seen what man can do*
*When the evil lives inside of you*
*Many are the weak and the strong are few*
*But with the water we'll start a new.*

*Well, won't you take me down to the levy?*
*Take me down to the stream*
*Take me down to the water*
*We're gonna wash our souls clean.*

After several beautiful minutes, her voice reverberating in the small studio, Wendy concluded with bluesy drama and we all realized what a special gift she had just given us.

"You all have washed your soul clean with the sweat of your body," she said as she walked to the door of the studio. "Now go out and have yourself a wonderful weekend."

Lying on our backs in *Savasana*, we all broke into spontaneous applause.

K ate and my plan for the rest of the day was to go cross-country skiing in Yellowstone National Park. We met up with friends Don, Lu, Gray, Steve, and Sonja and headed down through Paradise Valley to Gardner and the entrance to the Park. Between Gardner and Mammoth we came upon a dozen bighorns, including three or four with massive horns that challenged each other with headlong rushes ending in KABOOMs! that resounded off the canyon walls. Soon we saw herds of bison, and once a white mound, a bison covered with snow, that suddenly stood and shook the snow off, surprising us all.

Later, skiing out onto Blacktail Plateau, we talked about the sheer joy of this place called Yellowstone. I took photos as I often do, and soon fell behind while Kate pushed on and up far ahead with the rest of our party. Her strength has continued to grow and each and every day we both feel thankful for life.

To our left and right, in the trees and out on the open expanse of Yellowstone's Northern Range, we saw hundreds of elk, some near, some in the distance, all wary to our small group. Their wariness, we knew, came at least in part to their heightened sense of their own mortality brought on by the reintroduction of wolves to the Park some dozen years earlier.

Already, earlier in the day on the edge of Gardner, Don had spotted a lone black wolf trotting through the sage brush. Periodically here and now wolf tracks crossed the ski track we moved along, sometimes a lone set of tracks, sometimes in pairs. Looking down at one such track, and then looking up to see Kate and Gray skiing far off ahead, my mind drifted back to a year earlier—before Kate's surgery, before my Challenge.

It was a day much like this one: cold and crisp. Kate, Gray's wife Deb, and I had departed Bozeman early and we were the first to the trailhead. Three inches of new snow had fallen the previous night so the past day's ski tracks were covered. We pushed out into the fresh snow, soon breathing hard against the effort and opening coats to cool our sweat.

Within a mile, however, we were no longer breaking through fresh powder. Instead the trail in front of us had been trampled though not by the usual elk herds, but instead by wolves.

In places the wolves cut a swath thirty feet wide across the ski track. Wolf prints of all size and variety, going left, going right, but mostly going right down the trail corridor. For long periods the tracks would go straight up the trail, then one would split off to the right towards a set of pines, another split off to the left down a gulley. As we continued to ski sometimes the tracks disappeared altogether, only to reassemble in ones, twos, or maybe a group of six or eight all eventually re-meeting to continue up the trail.

We skied on, knowing that given the early morning snow the wolves were surely no more than hours ahead of us, maybe minutes. The tracks continued to come and go from the trail. I paused numerous times to take photos and soon Kate and Deb pulled far ahead, skiing with intent, heads down.

Suddenly, to my left perhaps a hundred yards away, a black wolf emerged from a set of trees and began trotting directly parallel to me, though moving slightly faster. Before I could get Kate and Deb's attention another wolf and then another, both gray, emerged into the open, also trotting parallel to us. I waved frantically at my ski partners, wanting not to disturb the wolves by yelling, though surely they were aware of us.

Kate and Deb skied on.

Finally, with six wolves paralleling us and the first two coming abreast of them, I whistled to Kate and Deb and pointed. They stopped dead in their tracks, mesmerized. I hurried up to join them and in the next few moments five more wolves appeared, all trotting parallel to the ski trail, unhurried but with intent.

We watched as the wolves pulled away from us, moving up an open hillside. One by one they crested the hill and disappeared. The last wolf was black, and it stopped on the hilltop to look back into the valley, to look back at us. After a majestic moment, the wolf turned and trotted off, heading on with purpose towards its next great challenge.

After an excited, "O-my-God-was-that-absolutely-incredible?!" moment, we did the same.

△ △ △

# A Note of Thanks

**M**any people had an impact on my 60-Day Challenge, as well as on this book. I will strive here to mention as many of them as I possibly can, but such an effort is surely destined to fail and I apologize to those that I inadvertently leave out.

I will start at the start, with my wife Katie Gibson, without whose love and support little matters. I appreciate your wisdom and honest feedback throughout the project, indeed throughout our lives together. I love you with all my heart. And my thanks to my Mom and Dad, who have always provided me a base to launch from, have pointed me in the right direction, and who have stood by post-launch with praise and support, or to pick up the pieces, whichever has proven appropriate.

Many folks gave of their time to read and review this work. The book's strengths emanate from the input they provided; its weaknesses are mine. Reviewers of early versions of the book provided important feedback to help me get rolling and I humbly thank them for their time. Those reviewers included Joan Exley, Deb Davidson, Mike

Yinger, Lu Goodrum, Linda Regnier, Betsy Buffington, and DeeAnn Diedrich.

I asked friends Kathy Brewer and Linda Ashkenas to do a bit more gloves-off review of a later version of the book. They had both helped me on a previous book so I knew what was coming…and knew it wouldn't all be good! Kathy provided superb input regarding direction and scope of the stories I was trying to tell. And she pushed me to think big about what I ultimately wanted the book to be for readers. Linda grabbed me by the ear and was not afraid to ask, "What on earth are you trying to say here!?" I have come to rely greatly on her candor and wisdom. I thank both Kathy and Linda sincerely for helping shape the book. I only hope that I moved far enough in the direction they proposed to overcome the shortcomings they pointed out.

I asked a number of Bikram instructors to review the book for errors in my representation or instruction of the poses. Thanks to Meg Latanzio, Chris Bunting, Rebecca Bunting, James Caldwell, Tony Brinks, and Emily Weinberg for taking time to look at the book through this lens and for providing valuable feedback (and to James, Tony, and Emily, plus Raina Plowright for cover reviews). I want to particularly and warmly thank James Caldwell for his strong editing efforts and wise feedback, much of which he provided while flying across the Pacific.

My sincere thanks to Randee Brinks for the use of her unique, beautifully conceived yoga pose icons. You can check out the full set of poses, not to mention the class schedule and happenings in Abbotsford British Columbia, at www.bikramyogaabbotsford.com.

I also want to acknowledge a number of Bikram Yoga studio owners from around the world that I had the opportunity to interact with through the course of writing this book:    Tamara Markatselis (Johannesburg, South Africa), Jennifer Lobo (New York City), Bill Thwaites (London), Karen Buckner (Dallas, TX), Radha Garcia (Boulder, CO), and Mary Jarvis (San Francisco, CA).

Over the course of my Challenge I had a number of instructors.  I would like to thank each of them for their passion for yoga; for their commitment to good physical, mental, and spiritual health; and for being the glue that holds their yoga community together.  I am hopeful that I have everyone and apologies if I miss anyone.  In Bozeman: Chris and  Rebekah Bunting, Meg Lattanzio, Wendy Westmoreland, Jessica Marsh, Lisa Wortman, Jackie Taylor, Susan Ramos, Even Howard, and Michael Barrett. In Corvallis:  Elizabeth Weber, Jeannie Niedner, Kacie Annis, Steve Hutzler, Erika Kraft, John Bassinette, and Alex Newport-Berra.   In Portland at John's Landing: Christy Whitney, Louis Stanley, and Jim Girod.   And finally I want to recognize several other instructors I had the honor of practicing under during the preparation of the book: Tavis Cline, Angel Colon, Afton Carraway, Crystal Slater, Noelle Kehoe, Kristyn Birrell, Kim Williamson, Emily Weinberg, and Billy Auclair.

Finally, I would like to close by naming, as best I can, the many, many Bikram Yoga classmates that I shared sweat and laughter with in recent years.  The list will without fail be incomplete and even where I have the correct names, I am sure that I will have misspelled many (how many variations on Kristen...er...Kristin...er...Cristina are possible, anyway?). Likewise I will hit multiple folks with one name as my brain is just not that organized to keep track of the total numbers (I think I have shared the studio with at least four Dana's, for example).

So thanks to all of you who have shared your positive energy with me in recent years, including Alba, Amy, Ben, Beth, Betsy, Bill, Bob, Bruce, Carl, Cathie, Casey, Chris, Cristina, Christine, Clark, Cornelius, Cory, Dan, Dana, Dean, Deb, Elliot, Eric, Erica, Fran, Genise, Guy, Gwen, Heidi, Holly, Ian, Ivy, James, Jeff, Jennifer, Joanna, John, Jon, Katherine, Kathleen, Kriste(i)(y)n, Kirsten, Laurie, Lori, Lu, Mary, Michael, Mike, Misty, Molly, Noelle, Paul, Putter, Raina, Rob, Sandy, Shane, Shannon, Shasta, Sherri, Stacey, Stanette, Stephanie, Steve, Suz, Tahnee, and Thomas.

Two final notes. First, I want to mention Tara, a classmate and friend to all of us that practiced Bikram Yoga in Bozeman over the last many years. Tara lost her life in a tragic explosion while at work one day. It was a shock to everyone: to her family and friends, to her Bikram community, to all Bozeman-ites. Tara seemed to always be at class whenever I popped in; no surprise since she rarely missed a day. She always waved and gave me a beautiful smile. Along with her husband and family, we all miss her.

And finally I want to recognize that my father passed away during the preparation of this book. I love you, Dad. I think about you every day and I am looking after Mom, just like we talked about.

# Author Bio

S cott Bischke lives in Bozeman, Montana, where he regularly continues his enthusiastic yoga practice. He previously published two books: <u>CROSSING DIVIDES: A Couples' Story of Cancer, Hope, and Hiking Montana's Continental Divide</u>, and <u>TWO WHEELS AROUND NEW ZEALAND: A Bicycle Journey on Friendly Roads</u>.

Along with his writing career, Scott has worked as a chemical engineering science researcher at three national laboratories, as an environmental engineer for Hewlett-Packard, as the lab director for the Yellowstone Ecological Research Center, and as a science and technology writer and facilitator specializing in Greater Yellowstone Area science and engineering issues.

Scott and his wife Katie Gibson have hiked, biked, and canoed in remote places in locations around the world including backpacking the length of the Continental Divide from Canada to Mexico, and hiking and canoeing the length of the Yellowstone River. A common thread in all of Scott and Katie's travels has been their desire to immerse themselves in the peace, solitude, and tranquility of the natural world. The couple seeks out people, places, and activities that reinforce their desire to live a life filled with positive energy. Perhaps more simply, they seek to live a life that reflects their gratitude for being alive each and every day.